Whistling Psyche

Fred and Jane

Sebastian Barry was born in Dublin and educated at the Catholic University School and Trinity College, Dublin. He published a number of books of poetry and prose until 1988, when his first play, *Boss Grady's Boys*, was produced at the Abbey Theatre in Dublin. Subsequent plays include *Prayers of Sherkin*, and three Out of Joint productions, *Steward of Christendom, Our Lady of Sligo* and *Hinterland*, all directed by Max Stafford-Clark. His novel *The Whereabouts of Eneas McNulty* was published in 1998 and *Annie Dunne* in 2002 (Faber). His new novel *A Long Long Way* will be published by Faber in 2005.

by the same author

plays
HINTERLAND

novels
ANNIE DUNNE

SEBASTIAN BARRY

Whistling Psyche
Fred and Jane

faber and faber

First published in 2004
by Faber and Faber Limited
3 Queen Square, London WC1N 3AU

Typeset by Country Setting, Kingsdown, Kent CT14 8ES
Printed and bound by CPI Group (UK) Ltd, Croydon, CR0 4YY

A CIP record for this book
is available from the British Library

0-571-22460-1

Contents

WHISTLING PSYCHE

Whistling Psyche was first produced at the Almeida Theatre, London, on 12 May 2004. The cast was as follows:

Dr Barry Kathryn Hunter
Florence Nightingale Claire Bloom

Direction Robert Delamere
Design Simon Higlett
Lighting Tim Mitchell
Projection Design Jon Driscoll
Music Ross Lorraine
Casting Maggie Lunn

Acknowledgements

I would like to acknowledge the poignant biography by
June Rose, *The Perfect Gentleman*, published in 1977 by
Hutchinson and sent to me by my uncle Desmond Barry
the following year, as being in his opinion about an
ancestor. I have been digesting its mysteries ever since.
Also that heroine of Irish history Cecil Woodham-Smith,
and her vivid biography *Florence Nightingale,* published
in 1950 by Constable; also the incredibly fleet and singular
chapter on Florence Nightingale in Lytton Strachey's
Eminent Victorians, published in 1918 but reading still
like a work of tomorrow. A much more recent book is
David Murphy's pioneering *Ireland and the Crimean War.*

Characters

Dr Barry
Miss Nightingale

*The waiting room of a Victorian railway station, fine
cast-iron struts and medallions, a row of red-plush
seats against the panelled wall, framed prints set into
it, travellers' scenes of Egypt, England, Ireland, Africa,
a portrait of Queen Victoria, a long mirror, et cetera;
but the edges of the room fraying into the evocative
decrepitude of a graveyard monument – wax flowers,
twisted lead, long-dried bunches of withered flowers.
There is quietness as ill befits a railway station, and
music runs along like confident rats.*

A fine clock shows ten minutes after two.

*There enters a figure, old, very small for a man, in
a fine, dark uniform. There is a helpful moonlight on
the features, and on his plumed three-cornered hat. The
face is anxious enough in this privacy. Barking of dog
off. The voice is sharp and high. The uniform is that
of an Inspector General of Army Hospitals, in the mid-
nineteenth century. But if this place has a time, it is
around 1910. The figure pauses at the doorway and
whistles back out into the dark, waits a moment.*

Dr Barry You will not need to be told, I am sure, of the
beauties and exactitudes of the poodle. For no animal, nor
hardly human either, exists on such a plane of delicacy.

A moment.

I have spent my whole life travelling, and I am not
surprised to find myself here. It is familiar. A pleasant
waiting room, undoubtedly in England, by the sheen and
the exactitude of it.

9

A moment.

My poodles have all been Psyches. I named the first Psyche, and could think of no reason not to give the same ticket to the second, and the third, for truly that ethereal animal is an image of my own human soul.

Looks about at the room, steers towards a chair.

I have an odd sense of having been here before. Not just once, but many times. Perhaps indeed it is not so pleasant. Is Nathaniel to hand? Sitting patiently in the third-class waiting room? And where is poor Psyche?

A moment.

It lessens the misery of a small death, to take up with a new creature at least of the same name. So that I might go out into the walled garden at night in the clean filth of the dark and call that same important name, *Psyche, Psyche,* whistling my eternal dog through the boles of the orange trees. Of course I speak of my old home in Cape Town. And be at the cake shop to buy the same little cakes that I might lay some small offering of delight at the altar of her nature, which is all delight.

Takes off the hat and sits, the chair emphasising how small the person is.

No poodle ever drew breath that was not an entrancement of thankfulness. There have not been many humans who on their passing have aroused in me a desire to replicate their presence by giving their names to another, even if that were possible, even if humans were to be purchased as handily as dogs, as indeed in those southern parts of Africa in my time was still more than possible, being in truth a staunch trade of the Cape and carried on by good British men, though under new names. But it was all the same thing. In fact a new human was easier got,

now I think of it, for I never received a poodle that had
not aged three months already by the time she reached
my arms, trembling and sweating with love on the Cape
Town shore, as the ship bearing that bundle of fur and
veritable twigs for legs, and the heart of a lion produced
by nature in miniature, hove into view from its eternity
of a voyage from old England. Thus bringing to me
again Psyche, renewed and familiar. Two Psyches long
I was in Cape Town, and I am sure there were many that
wished heartily I had only lasted myself but half a dog.

A moment.

A waiting room, a fragment of a house, where no one
lives, set down upon a platform . . . I think of that strange
orange light under the orange trees, in that high-walled
garden, near the mysterious African sea. The period of
my life I can with justice call happy. Myself in the big
wooden house, the linens on my bed as stiff as sails, my
little dog Psyche making a frolic of the heat. And my
servant Nathaniel arranging all things with his domestical
genius, buffing both house and master till we shone.
I think of the bewildered natives, the sick and the mad,
and the bewildered people of the colony, also sick and
mad, in different ways and manners. There was only
myself to stand between, to raise the black madman and
drive back the white, the one rattling in his given chains,
the other in the chains of his own invention, the horror
of the climate, the shortness of an English creature's life
there, the elemental emergency of the continuous sun.
But that I am that other sort of creature, neither white
nor black, nor brown nor even green, but the strange
original that is an Irish person, I might have had more
kin with those suffering whites. But my heart, my white
heart blackening secretly with age, was with the soiled
lunatics that cried out like large owls in the bright
asylums, as if the endless sunlight was hurting their eyes,

their souls. And the stumped lepers, and the heathen with livers boiled in makeshift drink, all the delirium tremens of the outcast and the forsaken, were in the upshot my purpose and my marvels. For in them only could I see the weaving of God, if God, that poor shaky character, there might be – in them only the origin of philosophy and the destinations of medicine. And I was a young army doctor, in the great muddled wool-basket of Empire.

A moment.

Good beginnings may have bitter ends. And I am of a mind that all I did, all I accomplished against the odds that clerks and administrations and their officials like to throw in the way of the tentative walk of progress, is as nothing now, no memorial to my days exists, no record of my intense and sometimes loving labours. Because I did not so much serve the civilised man and woman in their starchy trappings, but mostly applied myself to the despised and lonesome of the world, and there is no medal, preferment or honour to be got from such. It is a painful curiosity to me that a life of some seventy years can register so lightly in the annals of humankind. To the degree that such a life might blow off the page of the historian's manuscript like a shard of feather from his quill, before ever his ink recorded my efforts and monuments, even if such monuments are merely the prayers of destitute men recording that one time in their existence a single person in good clothes thought their welfare was worth more than a cavalry horse.

Takes out a thin black cheroot.

And more curious to me still that a person of the light character of Florence Nightingale – (*Strikes a lucifer.*) – the heroine of the Crimean War – (*Lights cheroot.*) – might now be remembered as if she were a royal

personage, when I, that took the same interest as she
in drains and cleanliness, and that twenty and thirty
years before her, am consigned to a footnote of imperial
oddities.

*Now there enters a woman in her eighties: tall, serene
like a monarch of shadows. She wears a long blue
skirt and starched blouse, with a rich Turkish-looking
jacket, all swirls of dark blue and dark red. She has a
strong, clear face, her hair pulled back tight, with a
richness in it, a confident brushstroke. She carries a
few little books in a ribbon, and a small wooden box.
She is as confident as a child in its own room. She
looks at the clock, checks it against her own watch.
But it still says ten past two.*

Miss Nightingale To the second. Perfectly in accord. (*to
Dr Barry*) Good evening.

*She finds a seat and sits pragmatically. Dr Barry pays
no heed to her.*

(*looking at Dr Barry*) He is very small. He does not wish
to see me. I do not think I know him, resplendent as that
uniform is. He does not like a woman to be travelling
alone, to be sharing something with his masculine nature,
even if it is just a room – this elegant little room. (*She
tries again.*) Good evening. Do you think it will rain
again? It has been raining all July, and it is a very terrible
business.

Dr Barry is studiously smoking.

No, he will not speak. He would rather pollute his
surroundings. (*looking about*) An anteroom? A waiting
room? It is apt.

A moment.

13

Dr Barry I hear something low and mean, like a broken music, like a nagging voice. But I cannot see where it comes from.

He gets up and paces up and down, smoking viciously.

Is it to my shame that I was born in the county of Cork in Ireland, in the year – many dark years ago? I am a creature of shadowed origin, in that my place of birth is insecure, dark, and better so. Cork constitutes itself in part of the best lands of Ireland, fat cows graze there, with fattening udders swinging gently, cows that are crazy in the afternoons to be driven back down the gradual hills, for to be relieved of that milk. They are musical cows, those cows of lower Munster, lowing with increasing panic as the sun fires down sumptuous and golden to the earth, like a religious queen, and comical, in that their panic is characteristic and easily allayed, so they are not tragic souls. That was the bucolic choral singing of my early babyhood, and in my heart at two or three were drawn the country maps, country places and country sounds and doings, when we would throw ourselves on the pleasant and easily given mercy of relations, who at the time ate with the plenty of princes and the disregard of millionaires. Because the land threw her bounty in their laps. And so things went on, plain and ordinary enough, until that hunger and pestilence leaped forth upon the same green fields with fang of wolf and embrace of bear, somewhere around 1810 or 12, when famine became the urgent lamenting of our history, and changed all things. The landed people turned their gaze inward because outward, upon the white roads of Ireland and in the mudded huts so like unto those later that I found in the rural plethoras of Africa, limbs withered to sticks and stenches of misery and terminality amassed themselves so that any possible scales of landlord and labourer were quite broken, and a bleak

nightmare beyond words took the place in the book of
life where once these old colonists and native rich had
tried by the grace of their Gods and the wilful toil of
their minds and limbs to make a rural idyll in their
inherited fields. These means and ambitions were routed
utterly by calamity, and hearts and souls of those with
plenty withered just as surely if more invisibly than the
real and true limbs of the destitute and poor. And in that
change I think I trace the beginnings of my true story.
For necessary then to all Irish persons was subterfuge
and subtle guiles, things not unknown to me now and
long since, things ever carried before the spectacle of my
private story like obliterating lights. But wherever in the
world I have found a version of Ireland, a palimpsest of
that once-easy kingdom, I have striven again to create
that old balance and medium among destroyed and
enmired peoples, as if by my qualities and doctoring
abilities I might restore to the earth a true translation of
the ancient text of Ireland's happiness, however forlorn
in the attempt, even however foolish and by civilised
people reviled for my instincts and dreams. For nothing
is more discommoding to the general stability and
luxuries of accommodated folk than the spectre of
change and the sword of reform that cuts through not
only the noisome horrors of what happens in the dank
margins of things, but also inevitably the sweet-scented
calicoes and poetries and philosophical affectations and
religious contentments of the officers and high servants
of a long-established and increasingly encushioned
Empire.

A long moment.

Perdition is my due, for I am – (*gazing in the long mirror,
touching the face a moment*) – I do not know, I do not
know. Oh, that I might have some sudden confidante,
but that is not likely now.

*Barking of dog. Turns head and looks towards the
door expectantly. Nothing. Crushes out the cheroot
underfoot, sits again.*

Miss Nightingale He seems anxious about that dog.
Perhaps it is his darling. An animal, though not destined
for God's heaven, may yet seem sometimes greater than
a mere person. I myself once loved a little owl, Athena.
She was like a tiny god, a tiny idol I suppose, as neat
and square as a soap-stone statue, and she would have
fitted in the palm of my hand, had I ever subjected her
to that indignity. It is not easy to itemise the attractions
of a little owl. She was the size of a clerical partridge –
if you will allow me the metaphor, for she was so like
a small, squat parson in a sort of dancing suit – but
sometimes I fancied the intertwining notions of the
universe itself passed through her mysterious skull. One
morning watching her, I thought of the Hill of the Skull,
Golgotha itself, in Jerusalem, and had the oddest inner
vision of three tiny crosses, with Christ between flanked
by his famous criminals. It is not healthy to see Christ
crucified on the head of an owl. And Athena was older
than that, as old as the goddess she was named for,
goddess of the state, of the city, of the power, goddess of
doing and artifice, even, yes, of war, a goddess of many
uses, immortal in her day but finite, finished now. My
little beastie, as creatures go so silent, unasking, sufficient
unto herself, elegant but plump, pretty but grotesque,
one in number but numberless, an image, an idea
representing the million Platonic owls of the earth,
sounding over the marshes and stirring the dreams of
poets and farmers. Little Athena, that required nothing
but a feed of mice and a thimble of water. When I was
called to go to the Crimea, in that great excitement and
sudden preparation, Athena was put in an attic to be
safe out of the way, and when all the baggage left, she

was forgotten for a few days, and died there of hunger and silence. My sister brought her to me and put her in my hand, like a tuppenny bag of salt, that the kitchen air has got into and made hard and damp. My poor little beastie. For her I cried. I do not for a moment imagine you think me a person that has cried often.

A moment, then in growing vexation:

Unless it was from sheer misery – the vexation of being denied the arena of my calling. And it was denied me because of course it was a strange calling. A nurse in my good mamma's day was a poor fallen type, heavy with fat and evil intent, consuming jars of noisome beer, neglecting her charges – women who themselves were abandoned to the sanitary horrors and terminal, dark corridors of the hospital itself, a place where visions became black and the depravity and the hopelessness of a sort of end of earth took hold on everyone. A nurse was the creature of that place, taking colour, cloth and manners from it, her soul, like the walls, running with sweaty moulds. So I, the daughter of wealthy people, with our five houses, our acres of carpets and lawns, our peacocks and our pride, could only fling the howling demons of fear and outrage into those cushioned domains. And they strove to hold me, to wrap me in the same dailysome rictus that held them, they would rather me stretched upon a third couch, like my sister and mother, prostrated by good fortune and rich food in those soundless mansions when Victoria was but a girl like me. So that they turned me into a wraith, a revenant unto myself, a coiling, crazed version of who I was, a bad likeness, an hysteric, a weeper, a fool, a philosopher of idleness, who could not eat, who could not speak except in dreams, where I raged against fine dresses, and cursed myself roundly like a soldier. And I bore those wounds gracelessly, and would not have balms put on them,

because cure there was none. Ravenous, strangely,
wandering the house ravenous, and not able to eat, as
I say, because it was not food I needed, but something
widening, something seething and guiding, like a
Bethlehem star, to bring me back into the world of birth
and death, not that horrible stifle of a life, that smothering,
mothering place where I mouldered, all loved and admired
and understood and as good as dead.

*She has been almost shouting. Glances at Dr Barry,
who pays her no heed. A moment.*

Dr Barry Lonesome.

A moment.

Ever thus. It might well be asked what conditionality of
being kept me at a distance from my fellows. For why
I was forever watching the passing show of life as if from
a platform of my own, alone like a grandee without equal.
There were times when I have come close to my fellow
man, as close as a person can get in fact without entering
one of the portals of the body. For I rescued in childbirth
the wife of an important nabob, with spread of orchards
and levees of working men, and a fear in his heart as he
watched indifferent nature storm against the frame of his
wife, as she strove to bring her baby into the darkened
world. Swift as a swift itself, as it enters its little nest of
clay, my hand with its blade as sharp as sea-grass, cut
into that grand wife, lifted her astonishing child from her
belly, where it lay in the first gifts of water and peace,
gave the hollering creature to my starchy nurses, sliced
the amazing chord that binds the two musics of mother
and offspring, and placed back the ruptured folds of
skin, and stitched that important lady together again,
quickly, quickly, because infection rushes in like invisible
water. She kept her privileged life, and the baby throve,
and was given my name for a name, the sweetest reward

I ever got for my labours. And at the christening in the
opposite of such haste, I held the little lamb, thinking
on its plight inside the womb, some unknown warnings
sounding there, with the urgency of threatening death.
I held it in my official arms, not betraying by my face for
a moment my intense pleasure, feeling in my own
innards an answering joy, as if I had brought this girl
myself out into the tricky light. With immense frowns
I felt that soft sparrow in her blankets rimmed with gold,
beating like a bird, vibrating like a drum. Its mother
gazed at me with open gratitude, the father in his mighty
clothes talked to me as if I were a sort of God who,
though queer and small to look at, was in a true guise
as expansive and important as the sun. Otherwise and in
more usual times I was forced by lonesome facts, too
sore to set out, to keep my distance from my fellow
Christians like a dog dubious of the teeth of its own
kind.

A turn of light, music. He goes to the door, whistles.
Stares out gloomily. Miss Nightingale gives up on
engaging Dr Barry, gets up, looks at the pictures,
and examines in particular a portrait of Victoria on
the wall.

Miss Nightingale She touched on everything but remained
untouched. Victoria. She saw the passing greatness of
poets and painters, ministers prime and minor, chancellors
and neurotic dukes, and everything was done for her,
through her, and of her, as if her true offspring were
liberties and progress, like the children of a virgin queen.
My, my. In Scotland, where I talked with her, she was
both everything ordinary and magical, there was an
absolutely silent music that attended her, of great courses
and profound decisions, a sense of ordering everything
not by sleight of hand, but by some impossible reach of
insight and empathy. If she was surrounded by those

gossiping courtiers, ninnies and nonentities, ever the
expanse of her mind was filled with the important
urgencies of the day, and I noticed the strangeness of that,
even how she fretted, and seemed to worry herself that
she might not do the right thing, how it overwhelmed
her for moments in sequence, so that she became silent,
and had the look of a panicking animal. As though the
effort of Empire were like a terrible illness that smote the
mind. And it seemed to me the mere things on her table,
the knick-knacks and objects, of a curious domestic or
imperial cast, were heavy, chosen for their heaviness,
because she wished them to anchor her down, keep her
table from floating away on her, born aloft by the gases
of doubt and danger, flying her out across the Thames,
across the Irish Sea, down to Africa and Asia and the Arab
worlds, all her subjects below labouring, suffering, dancing,
singing, imploring her to keep her mind on the eternal
question that reduces us all, what to do, what to do.

*Dr Barry looks back as if catching a trace of these
words.*

So that because of that essential grace in her nature she
listened to me when I brought her my account of Scutari,
and my understanding of the failure of the medical
systems then destroying her armies. She listened with
the eyes of a queen and the heart of a common woman.
She didn't tell me what to think, or resist in any way,
or defend her high officers in the manner they tended
to do themselves. So therefore, because she believed
me, she elected to think as I did, and transferred my
own thoughts to her vigorous mind and made them her
own, and acted out of them thereafter as if her name
in that respect was Nightingale. So when I bombarded
government and assailed ministries to gain my great
changes, I felt I had the subtle whip of her good wish.

Dr Barry Did I hear the detestable word Nightingale?

Miss Nightingale I wonder all the same what is the story of this old creature, talking to himself in his bitter little tones? Like the sharpest of lemon juice in a sweet dish. Mr Witherchops. Why is he here, with his eyes as black as liquorice, muttering viciously to himself? He may be grotesquely injured in the mind, by scenes of ferocious carnage too dark and drenched with blood to have kept his sanity. I should feel perhaps something for this old wretch. Or interrogate him professionally? Soothing music is a great balm to the mad. I know what I will do.

She raises the little box she brought in with her.

I will calm the poor fellow with this. Yes.

She opens the box and it begins to play a tune. She holds it up towards Dr Barry helpfully.
A moment. The moonlight toiling. Tin music.

Dr Barry In the machineries of Empire there may well reside compassion hidden like a gem in mud, but I have not seen much evidence of that glitter. The urgent histories of our times tell us again and again of the great mission of Christendom, expressly and momently to go to the plight of the heathen sunken in his philosophical slime. They speak elegantly of the spiritual horrors of little naked nations that have had the arrogance and rudeness to run their own paltry affairs inside the barriers of mountains and deserts, without the gentle and civilising guidance of that remarkable creature near kin to an angel, the European person willing to risk health and life to go out upon a colony and draw his pay so often merely for the dereliction of duty – to lend his healthful influence, should he happen to be a doctor, by confining himself to his handsome house, as if his expertise were an artful wind that might drift out over his orchards and his roses, and heal the sick and the lame by a magic far more unlikely than a heathen dance.

Miss Nightingale True, true, and doubly true, but are you not, little sir, one of those very doctors, to judge by your mighty garb, and your extraordinary hat?

Dr Barry The officers of Empire sit in their houses and then when they can do no better, visit each others' gold and resplendent houses by polite, if sometimes ironic, rota. It is those other lowly beings, the merest servants within Empire, our soldiers, our canal diggers, our labourers sent out to infect the native with this burdensome activity of labouring, that perform the true work and meet the actual dangers. So you will conclude immediately that it is these noble souls, so selfless and so inconsiderate of their own health – who if they take refuge in cheap alcohols yet suffer the murderous delirium tremens for their pains, or end up in the madhouse crying out for their hurt heads to be healed – you will say that it is these lovely souls that Empire strives to honour and nurture. By this fashion we effect it: soldiers in barracks without clean air or linen, with the foulest slop for food, without vegetable or fruit, who die in their thousands of diseases rather than of wars, who come out to dark places with their bright English and Irish and Scottish faces, and endarken there and die without help or hindrance or pity from any powerful man.

Miss Nightingale Halleluja, sir. I echo you.

Dr Barry I saw in Jamaica whole companies of men depart this earth, from lack of an open window in a barracks, a decent drain, or a single apple. It is little it would seem for a governor to suffer the awful death tolls of the solders in his districts, who writhe and cry out in agony, despair and die, and though this may trouble the human dreams of him that steers such worthless hearts,

what a brave, gay face the governor shows in the evenings
at parties and levees, wearing the golden uniform and
the plumed hat with an admirable show of courage and
endurance. But that is the wisdom of authority, to remove
itself from pestilence and work. For work, especially the
work of an empire, is deadly and done to a short song.
Yet it is oddly true that a suffering man shows oftentimes
grace. You may tend a tormented lunatic that in some
sudden instance exhibits a redeeming gentleness of soul.
For shining out of ruined people are the remnant parts
that ill luck and short rations and indifference cannot
destroy. Even the direst madman in his last extremes may
for a moment calm and look at you with the fiercest
love, as if in your face he sees for that moment an
amalgam of the people he has loved, undoubtedly in
better times, and in the broken mirror of your features
spies his lost lovers, his father, his mother and his kin, if
it should so happen they were gentle to him and looked
on him with the especial notice of those that could
describe his characteristics like vivid poets, like the very
Shakespeares of his individual life. And in that glance is
the purpose of this earth's journey, if any purpose there
is, and when priests and ministers blithely invoke the
soul, perhaps they have oftentimes forgotten that the
greatest soul ever seen upon the earth belonged to
a wandering vagabond half-mad with memory and
mission that preached what seemed a ludicrous fallacy
of a religion, and thought his own low-born body, the
mere thrown-together limbs of the son of a provincial
carpenter, would be the saving of mankind if expressed
in biscuit form and taken once a week at a gathering of
like-minded fools.

Miss Nightingale Oh, this is dark. There is scandal here.
There is creeping changes, and apostasy unchecked, and
a crossing over. And I admire it.

Dr Barry For these views I may add I was distrusted, diminished, and at last dismissed.

Miss Nightingale You do not surprise me.

Dr Barry I attempted to cross over those immense barriers, those mountains of obscurating philosophies and one-sided histories, that separate the likes of myself from such souls without acknowledged stories or importances. What assisted me in this flight from position and all the usual structures, mental and actual, of grandeur, was I should think the strange mixture of scenes observed throughout my babyhood in Ireland, where the dividing line between opulence and cold cries of hunger was sometimes only a meagre hedge, or that ironical construct known as a ha-ha, where a falling ditch invites an illusion of connection between a genteel lawn and a plethora of struggling fields. Those visions of childhood were more deeply poetical to me than the satirising of one even so great as Alexander Pope, who loved nothing better than an antithesis to point up the horror of difference in society, though mine was a poeticality without the usual recourses of that trade, since it lacked pastoral easiness and was utterly devoid of harmony. Rather it was a jangling of destructed metres, the cries and the worse silences of those that hunkered in weeping cabins, and the laughter and polite, useless talk that passed the strange Irish time for the grandees of Cork, though some of them it is true were loveable and astute.

Miss Nightingale This is horribly familiar and unfamiliar in the same breath. These are thoughts that afflicted me too, *mutatis mutandis*. But to think them is one thing – to speak them out, even in this strange place, is an epilepsy of misdemeanour! And yet, and yet . . .

Dr Barry This is the haziest part of my recollection,

in that I have been driven in my mind to befog and becurtain such early days that lacked an ambiguity proper to my status now, yet out of that dampening mist and forceful if cloudy horror rose my proper character, with eyes so open they wept in the sunlight, and heart so seared it could do no other than prompt a lifetime of resistance and revolution. Whether I effected anything, or turned any system over that was irredeemably hostile to the happiness of the madman and the sick, or the entire lack of happiness I should say, is a question that would haunt me if I did not acknowledge to myself, though it is written in no history and brought me nothing but an absence of advancement and eventually a dark old age, that according to my lights, cold and frightening Irish lights though they may have been, I raised a cry for the helpless; and when my cry went unheeded, largely, I set to to put a poultice on the sores of the leper by my own hands, and tried to manufacture a balm of circumstance for those souls like blasted gardens that were in residence in the foul imperial residences of the mad.

Miss Nightingale Evil opinions, but I must confess, they have a dark undertow of truth in them, and I cannot entirely refute them. Alas, poor Victoria. This is a suspect, singular, and weirdly irreducible person, and I should . . . But let me wind the box again.

She holds up the box.

Dr Barry My poor mother was a woman called Mrs Bulkley and you will feel a secret surprise when I call her so and cannot retrieve her familiar name, nor that more dear and secret name by which a child calls for its mother. My father is a dark blank, and if my mother spoke of him, the news and chronicle of his existence lodged nowhere in my childish head. I think I believed

as a child that I had sprung wholesale from my mother
without interference from any other agent, like a bleak
little angel or an accident, like food drops from the
mouth of an ancient, because he has neither teeth nor
strength to keep it in. I fell I thought from my mother's
mouth like a mumbled crumb, and grew at her side in
some solemn and inexplicable manner, until the day
I found my legs, and could trot beside her as we moved
in increasing panic from kin to kin. As it was in once-
resplendent houses that we found brief havens, such
places as groan with the weight of rain in their old walls,
and whose costly trappings feed the secret night-time
rats, there was always a room of shelves with the
ingredients of a magnificent education never looked at
and never opened on its walls, for my people were a
people that would nod towards learning as a fine mystery,
but not stain their natural minds with reading, and it
was the dashes across the countryside on huge muscled
hunters that intoxicated them, and the eating of great
meals when there was the money to invent them, and
the zealous marrying of fortune to fortune no matter the
ugliness of the bride or the horrible stricken features of
the bridegroom. Nevertheless it was in those mildewed
and mouldering rooms that I stole my education, so that
at the age of eleven I was preposterously over-read, and
knew the long history of the world better than aught else.
Humanistically roaming in the old woods of Tacitus, in
the courts of Cicero, and the happy miseries of Catullus,
I became a freakish child that no Irish drawing room
certainly could understand, for I would not speak of
geldings and mares and stallions, but metres, empires, and
Horatian irony, so that my every word was contemplated
as a horror and a sort of devilish manifestation. Indeed
and I do believe at this distance those poor simple Irish
squires and their wives must have thought I was speaking
in the tongues of Babel, or the drivel of the mad.

Miss Nightingale is attentive.

My mother Mrs Bulkley kept me by her, so I suppose
I can assume she bore some feeling for me, although
I do not remember her expressing it in particular, in the
manner of, *I do love you, my dear,* or the like, that
people depend on in their memories as the foundations
of their fortitude in the long watches of adulthood with
all its attendant hopelessness and diminishment. For how
soon it is we lose the wings of childhood and begin to
stand shriven and cold in the alleyways of the earth with
wingless backs.

Miss Nightingale Plato based his philosophy on the soul,
my mother on the sofa. Indeed she based herself on it.
She wished my sister Parthenope and myself to do likewise.
The three of us on three rafts amid the enervating flotsam
and jetsam of our great riches. She wished to be allowed
to lie, and to be inserted at length into the maw of death,
horizontally, like a letter into a letterbox.

A moment.

Dr Barry When my mother could no longer ignore the
growing fact that the kinspeople upon whom we
descended with all the grandeur of field mice were
persisting in increasing desolation of spirit and destitution
of purse, her panic proportionately increased. She resolved
at last to bring us to London where her brother, at least
in her own mind, existed in some state of abundance
and fame. Certainly even I knew the splendour of his
reputation, in that he was held by the nations in general
to be an adornment to English painting, the fact of his
origin in Cork perhaps not purposefully underlined. Be
that as it may, this strange person was grievously loved
by many of the great minds of those days, the foolish
Goldsmiths and the monumental Johnsons, all those men
that in my childhood gave lustre and meaning to being

alive in this world, giving worth to the celestial candle of the soul guttering in the decrepitudes of evident things by their powers of poetry, painting, and posturing.

Miss Nightingale This remnant person may not deign to speak to me, but he is a philosopher.

Dr Barry Be that as it may, my uncle James was identifiable as a sort of visionary of both women and Catholics, in that he had inserted both in his monumental paintings without the usual attendant ironies and idealisations or reductions. What we did not know then was that he had impoverished himself in the process, ironically principally in the creation of that vasty series before which mortals wondered and quailed, the 'Progress of Culture', in the rooms of the Royal Society of the Arts. As for the progress of my mother and myself, we made a cruel crossing, she in her tattered silks and cloak, me in my whittled outfit like a miniature or a smudge of hers, so that I must have appeared to those living people of England, in those lost days, as her shadow, her double, traipsing onto the bleak barren ship that plied between the islands. The heart is changed by the journey across England, and although on a map there does not seem too great a distance between Southampton and London, yet the visions and practicalities of that country alter many things in the clock of an Irish soul. The part that is familiar dismays, the poverty of the under-people and all their ways, and the new things, the grandeur of the things that are rich, strangely appal, as if there is something unnatural and uncanny about such raging wealth. In Ireland the people may consider themselves ill-served by their masters. But England is far worse, for the tremendous arrogance of the ruling lords is visited upon their own kin and kind, in essence, and nowhere is this more unseemly and bizarre than that revelatory journey though the bitter edges of London, the great ribbons and

ropes of her streets, the toothless Leviathan of poverty
that lies across everything, like a very whale itself issuing
forth no discernible cry, yet producing the semblance of
a terrible music. But how clean the cloths of the rich,
how costly, how rinsed and scrubbed their houses, to
such a degree that even at twelve I could sense the
cowering in my mother's spirit as she advanced upon
her brother's house, where I am sure she expected to
be deluged by the force of his possessions. Yet in the
upshot we came on a strange skeletal dwelling, a sort
of provisional place, with many storeys and rooms
certainly, but every one empty and cold.

Miss Nightingale This is quite a lengthy history and
I am afraid I must sit down again if I am to hear you
out. Please do not think it disinterest on my part. I am
after all close to ninety years of age.

*She retreats to her place, sits gratefully. Dr Barry is
seemingly unaware.*

Dr Barry My uncle stood in a kind of admirable rage
at the top of his steps, as if the coming of his sister were
yet another in his catalogue of daily catastrophes, the
horror of this Tuesday. He cried out to us in his addled
voice, like a creature caught in an iron tooth, that he had
not one bite of cheese to feed himself, and slept on his
bare floors. He looked or rather glanced hysterically at
myself, as if I were the bloom of leprosy or the carbuncle
of the plague, or a sprite of doom and misery from the
stories of his Irish childhood. He did not kiss his sister,
he recoiled from her in a windy grandeur of dismay. My
mother, as was her habit in these habitual humiliations,
wept at my side, but silent as a stone, her tears nearly
forced inward behind her cheeks by her horror and self-
shame. To stand in a London street being repulsed by her
own brother was to her the highest point of our ruin.

And we were as surely driven back as if his hatred were
an army, and all that evening wandered those streets,
feeling like ghosts of ourselves. In the fresh limits of the
small hours we found the strange solace of a district of
the Thames, and sat there in a little genteel park, where
there were seats for the nursemaids and nannies in the
English daytimes, and for the first and last time in my
life my mother clutched me to her and stroked my hair,
whether as comfort to me or to herself, or both, I could
not tell, and in that sudden anguish of ironical delight,
did not ask, for fear of disturbing that unexpected bird
of mothering.

A moment. The little music.

I do not know how it happened, but patrons of my
uncle, hearing the story perhaps even from his own lips,
were horrified on his behalf. If he did not have an
affrighted soul, they posited one on his behalf. Small
boys were sent over London to find us, and perhaps
never would have, except that a deluge fell on London
that day, and my mother sat on beside the river without
moving us to shelter, a woman of some smartness with
a young consort, in the silver lines of rain, a conspicuous
enough sight to arouse the suspicions of a running boy
inspired by the promise of two shillings for his pains.
And so we were rescued and brought to the house of
a General Miranda, whose middle name I still carry in
remembrance of that remarkable gentleman. With that
miraculous Irishman Edmund Burke and the strange
Lord Buchan, he comprised a trinity of patronage for my
eccentric uncle. Comfortable of stature, he was one of
those beings contented only with a certain epicality of
life. The domestic engulfed him and made him fearful.
He was a kind of hero of freedom in his native South
America, and indeed in later years died there splendidly
for that cause. As my mother made no progress of any

sort in the following months, eventually the poor soul
was placed in an asylum, as it was thought in those days
for her own good and safety. I lay in my bed in the
General's house and hoped it was so, that my mother
might have found refuge from her hopeless distresses in
such a dark and blackened place. I never saw her again.

*A moment. Miss Nightingale closes the lid of the
music box with a snap. She is drifting asleep.*

The General was left then with the puzzle of what to do
with me. By a curiosity of history it so happened that he
was greatly interested in the freedom not only of South
America, but that other country so long in chains of
habitude and contempt, the lost fields of womanhood.
If he had incarcerated my mother Mrs Bulkley, he would
it seems liberate me like the serf of a terrible empire,
or a slave of received understanding. He knew, of course,
that I had a head of some unusual brightness, thanks to
those dilapidated libraries of Ireland. My hands were
thin-fingered and strong, and perhaps better for his plan,
I was rather unusual and angular in face, with sharp
features that could translate easily enough into the realm
of another sex. And so, adding everything up, and being
a military man himself, he arranged to send me in young
man's clothing to Edinburgh, to read to be an army
doctor. I was only just thirteen. He can be regarded
therefore as the author of myself. He gave me my names,
James for my uncle, Miranda his own addition, and my
poor mother's maiden name to round the invention off.
As I say these things, it suddenly strikes me as remarkable
enough that I do not remember now my original name,
so complete was the General's authorship. As that male
jacket closed over my chest, and those trousers engulfed
my thin legs, some other hidden blanket suffocated the
fire of a conventional future, where it might be I would
have enjoyed the love of another human person and the

boon of children born in the shelter of that love. The
garb of a girl was taken from me, item by item, and my
wardrobe of dresses, stockings and privy garments, scant
though it was, discarded for ever. And another far stranger
future began, where I was a creature in disguise among
the open landscapes of the Empire.

*A moment. The music box is loosened from Miss
Nightingale's sleeping fingers. It starts to fall, she
wakes to catch it.*

Miss Nightingale Oh! Forgive me, I slept. An old
woman sleeps everywhere. It is grotesque. And by God's
good heart, I was listening, listening. Oh, the frustration
of it. This man has suffered. He finds himself alone. But
no more than myself. I suppose he would take no interest
in my story, as being the history of a privileged and
wealthy person, and English into the bargain. Mothers
and babies were his topic, I think. Oh, my poor Sir Harry,
and the temperate offer of his hand! Sweet Sir Harry,
with his scholar's face and his skin as queer as a teacup.
Oh, I knew what motherhood could be. He had scanned
the annals of Livy, I the terrifying annals of midwifery.
Confinement after confinement like a sentenced criminal,
and perchance at some bleak break of day, among the
weakening light of the candles, to die in a shrieking
moment, trying to bring forth just such another as
yourself into these ruined realms. A private soldier had
a better chance of surviving his battles! When my kindly
Sir Harry Verney wished to marry me, I thought I could
not complete my moral character in such circumstances.
No, though I loved him well enough, and more. Perhaps
that was a kind of death, too. Oh, motherhood I know
nothing of in that personal manner. All my will was bent
on – fame? Forgive me do if I speak of the filth of fame
but there is nothing in it that can improve the heart or
appease the general derelictions of being alive. And that

is all I will say for the fame that my peculiar life has
brought me. Fame is proper to the dead, let them warm
themselves with it in the frigid graves, with the iron ivy
and the leaden leaves. Let it be something to ease the
waits of eternity, till the last trumpet sounds out across
the bleak and blackening stars, rousing the buried souls
of all the diminished shires. Let the grounds open with
a harvest of the forgotten great, their skulls like Irish
potatoes, wreaked by the famines of fame.

She laughs to herself.

Some months back they came with a medal in a box and
laid it on my lap. I could not speak to the matter. They
looked down at me kindly, and explained in slow
phrases what it was, the Order of Merit, bestowed on
me by our King. Pityingly they stared, they knew I was
befuddled in my mind and by senility sentenced. They
smiled at me as if I were a child, the more to be valued
now because my wits were gone. But the words were
hiding in my tongue, my room became a bell jar of
infinitely deep design, the ocean of ordinary life seemed
dim and vast, I could not swim up to them in their
vigour and certainty, but faintly signalled, faintly drifted,
like a tiny mollusc without eyes or soul.

A moment.

But in my days of vigour, before age put her hand upon
me, satirising my former self, I had the gallop and reach
of a giraffe. *(to Dr Barry's back)* You may think that a
ludicrous comparison, and that I intend to mock myself
by it. But I urge you, when next you can, to gaze on
that wonderful creature. She can do no other but reach
higher than her fellow creatures, she is strangely comely
and slender, maidenlike, but large as a dream, an animal
stretched out and altered in the most fantastical manner.
So you see I intend to give myself a compliment by

conferring on myself the emblem of that beast. In my days of vigour – great events. The troops advanced on Alma, covering those Crimean slopes with the harvest of the dead. They cried out in anguish, their fellows prosecuted the advance, and all England wondered that such men, with such low repute, could manifest such courage. The Light Brigade made its historied charge, those gallant men calling out to the enemy like veritable lovers, their swords held high, six hundred horses beneath them, trying to cross the sere terrain. And the greater fragment of that company was destroyed, right onto the enemies' guns they threw themselves, and bullets removed their exigencies and their dreams of life. In the aftermath it is said even the opposing Russian gunners stood amazed, and did not know whether to weep or wonder, and did both. Scores upon scores of horses without their riders now grazed the bloodied swards in a vision of agricultural hell. And it was not this extraordinary instance of the courage of British men that was my salvation, but the thing that happened next. Better to be a Frenchman in that murderous time, with their excellent hospital in Constantinople, but our own establishment in Scutari was the dark fate of our wounded men. And because the terrible news of that place of wrenching death reached England, by mercy of the correspondent of *The Times*, there was an outcry among the normally inert people, and it so happened that I was asked with the urgency of despair to go out there with a troop of nurses. My moment was arriving with the strange fanfare of a thing long desired and I reached out to meet it. The trenches were now dug under Sebastopol, the releases and dramas of conventional battle were over, the troops filled the trenches, and something disgraceful and dismaying began its reign. No provision had been made for supplies to feed the men, winter clothes to protect them were unprovided,

and it was as if no one on this dear earth existed to
rectify the matter. There were no battles now and the
generals were paralysed and annulled. Quartermasters
wrote their forms and the forms were countersigned and
nothing happened, except a typhoon endlessly turning of
paperwork, and that could not feed the troops. Because
there was nothing at the end of the chain except the
leaping bear of hunger and disaster. A fearsome winter
froze those bleak domains. The wounded were daily
embarked in ships across the bay to Scutari, where we
found the hospital intended to receive them, a fine old
place from the outside with four majestic towers. Inside
were corridors and long rooms without ending, the men,
roaring and calling, dying and rotting where they had
been deposited, in rows of beds tightly pressed together.
By a calculation of the hospital, its size, and the number
of beds, I quickly judged that there were in effect fully
four miles of them, four miles of British men, Scottish,
Irish, English and Welsh, in dank rooms without air, and
in every room were two great vats where the urine and
the faeces of the soldiers were put, and the first thing
that met us when we entered was the wild broken music
of that stench, wedded to the gross heavy smell of
gangrenes and other suppurations. To this sensate music
was added the extraordinary music of human pain, the
bellowing, the cursing, the crying. It was to this that the
army had sent those soldiers that had put such wonder
and pride in British hearts. Little filthy tales were
circulating. Everything was rumour and fancy. But I think
it was true that those very horses since so honoured by
the metres of Tennyson went quite without fodder, and
thinned and famished and died every one, to the eternal
disgrace of this country. Some froze where they stood,
like mocking statues. For not a blade of straw or grain
of oats was there for them, their wounds also were
ignored in the bleak dullness of official minds. I would

tell you, if you were only listening, that the reason why
such disasters befell the Light Brigade was because the
two commanders, an Irish grandee and his English
brother-in-law, could not agree, by dint of old histories
could not be friends, could not even communicate by
underlings, let alone speak to one another, were both too
petty in their minds to . . . But no, let me not adapt an
Irish song to an English tune. Perhaps it is that the gift
of the mind of those that rule, in England or anywhere,
is to engender miseries! Often and often I think of those
horses, I know not why, thinning and famishing in the
dark aftermath of the most famous and revered action
in the annals of that war. But at any rate – the Turkish
orderlies would not empty the vats of excreta, so when
they were full they overflowed, sending their writhing
tides along the rooms. Rats frolicked in the corners,
thinking a wonderful charnel house had been created
for their enrichment, as indeed it had. Never did doctor
or other officer go near the men, once a soldier was
wounded he was of no account, because in those times a
soldier was nigh equal a mere beast, being considered to
be the refuse in the first instance of society, the dullards
and the drunkards of every British town, London,
Dublin, Belfast and Glasgow, and the very detritus of the
countryside. In that at least we were united, England,
Scotland, Wales and Ireland! And I and my women could
do nothing but wait till we were asked to intervene.
The doctors in charge were in a black state of rage and
despair. They were in fear of losing their positions and
did not understand the outcry in England and what it
meant for them. A terrible time ensued where we were
witness to impossible pains, as peculiar choleras swept
the wards, very like to that famine fever in Ireland that
took pauper and prelate alike. The doctors were like
cooks boiling cabbages till they were green slime,
everything was late and nothing was soon. I examined

the drains as was my wont and interest and was
astounded to discover that the outflow of the system had
long blocked up, so that every effluent, every noisome
and poisonous seeping, merely added itself to a vast core
of similar discharges, and then spread out through the
very stones and mortar of the hospital, rising back up
through the building like a murderous rain, and its gases
and hissing vapours poured down through vents and
orifices back onto the long, doomed rows of men. We
were killing our men ourselves, not by the bullets of the
Russians or the Turks, but we were bringing them to
death by the blithe ignorances and lethal dither of those
official men. It was in that waiting time, before we were
allowed our way . . .

Dr Barry (*breaking in*) I do not know what time it is.
It is dark out there among the platforms. I can hardly see
them. In the distance gas burns in the lamps along some
lonesome streets of Empire. I wish some happenstance
could rescue me. What time is my train? Where is it
bound? From whither comes it? What station of the
English night is this? A person tells stories because he
does not wish the wave of silence to drown him.

A moment. Dr Barry is agitated.

Lonesomeness is built on the shore of madness, the cure
for it is the great stretching sea of dementia itself. Let
me without further delay tell you the story of the fate
of that delightful man, Major Barnes. Who came out to
the colonies with a fervour I recognized in that he was
one of those who loved the earth and her beauties,
whether savage or civil, and though of a dark unhappy
nature in himself, yet could feel much comfort from the
grand explosions that were our Cape Town sunsets, and
though he wept as I did myself to see the little dark-
skinned babies washed up on the tides of the town beach,

little scraps not needed by their needy mothers, girls
themselves only puppies in a world of brutal dogs,
though he wept, did Major Barnes, yet he put himself
passionately to his engineering works, raising interesting
edifices all about the environs of Cape Town, bridges
with little Venetian-looking towers at either end, beautiful
canals of delicately trimmed stones that brought good
water out to heat-parched farms. The governor, just as
he was by me, was innately disturbed by the energy of
this man, and yet at the same time gave way to him, and
tried to supply the great sums of money that Major
Barnes required and often for the turning of Cape Town
into what he called a perfected paradise. Major Barnes
was a small person with much fat all about himself and
a red face from the quantities of Scottish beverages that
he was wont by his depressive nature to find solace in.
He was really an ugly little creature and wore his uniform
in a way that suggested strongly that the seamstress and
tailor had despaired of his unusual shape. Yet he was a
hero in my eyes, and he would drive me out in his carriage
to see his latest marvel, whether it might be a neat
square lighthouse on some murderous point, or a section
of the land made verdant and Edenic by his marvellous
knowledge of water. Would he had been able to stick to
water, and take refreshment in his achievements. But
Major Barnes was a gentleman running on the spot,
and after some years passed his mind descended into
alcoholic delirium and he was incarcerated in the town
asylum. Once there all trace of position and elevation
soon departed, I am sure. It so happened that it was
some months before I was able to go and see him, indeed
I would have thought him quite safe among the mercies
of that institution, given the transformations he had
effected in that far-from-perfected paradise of the city.
But no, what I found astonished me, and brought home
again to my heart what a cheat and an actor madness is,

for instead of my clumsy, podgy major, I found in a filthy
cell a thin dark creature without clothes or sense, raving
in a corner and eating the mortar from between the
ancient walls like it was sweetmeats. No one had thought
to clean him, as I suppose would have been a twice-daily
task, in that poor Major Barnes had no qualms now but
to defecate freely like a beast of the fields and pissed like
a donkey where he might at that moment stand. On his
face was attached a vicious red beard, and it seemed
to me also that the body hair that he may have been
afflicted with in ordinary life had also begun to grow, so
that he presented himself as a human being gone almost
over the verge of bestiality. What the governor, if he had
ever thought of setting his shining boot inside the
asylum, which he never did, would have thought of his
clever major now, I do not know. More horribly still, his
arms were tied harshly behind him so that he might not
do himself injury, and so he ate the mortar with his bare
face, snatching at the stuff with his teeth, like a dog.
Naturally I spoke to him, to see if in the miasmas of his
mind there might not be a remnant island of sense, but
there was not. (*walking up and down in agitation*)
I ordered him to be washed as often as required, his cell
kept clean, his little window opened to the light outside,
a loose gown to be given him and replaced as often as
he tore it, and his arms freed. I gave him for three days
the best-looking of the attendants, to read to him from
the books I found at his quarters, in particular the
adventures of *Gil Blas,* and this she did, and at the
end of the three days when I visited, he no longer
roamed and raved, but did his business in a pot like
any other mortal, and though he could not speak sense,
yet whistled and sang while the girl read out to him
those chapters so interesting to him. And this regime
I was anxious to apply to all those inmates that might
find succour in it, and asked the governor for money

that might effect it, and this he supplied readily, when I described to him the horror that Major Barnes endured. So that the Major, even in his diminished and ruined state, yet brought a change upon the wastes of that building, and even in madness caused to be brought in a breeze of beauty and relief, as if he might by force of the fineness of his soul, throw a tincture of paradise into the cauldron of that hell. When I left Cape Town some time after, of course I was informed by my remnant spies that the asylum soon reverted to its former condition, its darkness, its filth, and its neglect. The windows were sealed up again, and its sad inmates returned to the manners and hours of horror. And the officers of that asylum were allowed to return to their murderous idleness, and all was right with the world of Empire, in all its hopelessness and eternity.

A moment.

Miss Nightingale That is very true, all of it, but as I was trying to say, it was in that waiting time, before we were allowed our way –

Dr Barry (*breaking in again*) Every medical officer may have duties to which he cannot attend. Distance, a lack of roads, catastrophes, ravines, may bar his progress out to various afflicted peoples. And these impediments become enshrined as tradition, and so things go on, in the general chronicle of neglects.

Miss Nightingale I just wished, I simply desired, to finish what I was saying –

Dr Barry One such was a sorry place called with some ironical flair Heaven and Earth, a leper colony sited deep within the back districts of the Cape. Long realms of high trees, plunging rivers, long snakes, seemed reasons enough to leave those lepers to their own devices, attended as they were by three permanent staff, displaced Germans of some kind in this case. But it is not in my nature to allow the story of such a place to go on unmolested by my presence, and it would be difficult to forget the abysm of sorrow and simple human pain that I saw there when first I penetrated those convenient trees. The three attendants, low slovenly people all, lived some distance from their care in a low flat wooden house, and the children of the lepers attended them there as servants, and I believe worse, and when they showed at length the signs of their parents' disease, were ejected back into the maelstrom of the colony and abandoned. The parents, with their stumpy arms and bruises, their noses rubbed off by reason of their skins being entirely insensate and indifferent to blows and knocks, as if their skin alone were blind in the blaze of day, were like the drawings of artists constantly being rubbed out by mildews and time, God's mastery of line and dignity made inept by that fearsome affliction.

Miss Nightingale (*plaintively*) I just wished to finish. I think I am your senior by some years. No one could be as old as I. You should listen. I am perhaps accustomed to being listened to.

Dr Barry There were young women there of incomparable beauty and youthful grace, cast down in the deeps of sorrow by that slow erasure and extinction, and they knew that many years of horror stretched ahead.

Miss Nightingale Even in my senility, I am sure you should listen.

Dr Barry Nothing whatever had been done for these ruined souls, their limbs were decked in rags, their wounds untended and their needs unknown.

Miss Nightingale Senility, so-called.

Dr Barry With what heavy reluctance those three Germans put themselves to their tasks. I ordered by my unavoidable authority the entire sprucing out of that encampment, and the proper dressing of the people, and the education of the afflicted young, so that they might have a music of the imagination to help them bear their hopeless fates. And I begged the governor of the colony to allow me to release the children with no signs of leprosy, that they might be placed back carefully in the town, with gentle choosing among the blacks, but this it seemed raised only thoughts of nightmare and death in such minds. I did smuggle out one lovely boy and placed him in secret in my own orange grove, in a little neat hut, and for many years he lived there, and tended the trees with great exactitude, and that was a fine person I named Jim, not so much after myself but my uncle, the painter, that was a man as I have said as neglectful of his dress as any depressed German in an African forest, but also with a mind of colour and form so magnificent that all who knew him at least allowed him their admiration and their love, if he didn't bite back that love with his tongue as bitter as aloes. For in his composure of that orchard, in the clipping and pruning back of trees and the watering of those thirsty oranges, my own Jim was a perfect artist and in league with the suspicions and intimations of God. Meanwhile I would surprise betimes my three Germans, who of course were anxious that some morass would swallow me up or a new posting obliterate me, so that they could return to their whiskies and cards in their low house and let the lepers in their care be damned.

Miss Nightingale That is very beautiful, about the boy Jim, I will allow.

A moment. Very privately, intimately:

Dr Barry It is not beyond my notice, the rumours that have bedevilled me all my life. I know I was called the little wife of the governor –

Miss Nightingale puzzled.

– all these dark things I know. It would insult me and insult you not to declare it. And who am I talking to, in this imperial darkness?

A moment.

There is something provocative of rumour about a person locked in mystery, a person that can dance and talk and amuse and yet seek no mate, with a uniform of incomparable neatness and exactitude, and small I suppose for an army man, and a voice of some troubled timbre, who is brave and can penetrate into districts of desolation like a pilgrim that knows no dimness of soul, who can carry themselves in the company of governors and paupers equally, and I suppose most tellingly, needs no one else except a poodle and a fine heart like Nathaniel at their side, that excites not only story and the mealy mouths of gossip, but also I think, and I fear to exaggerate though it strikes me as true, a kind of hidden lust. As if to possess such a person would be a kind of obscene ravishment, as if to imagine unclothing me, revealing me, opening me like a parcel hidden long underground, like a box said to contain jewels and deeds that will make the discoverer rich as Croesus, would be in effect to be driven mad with passion and then launched to a new pitch of sanity by its wild satiety. Certainly there were women in those lost colonies of the world, in Cape Town rooms polished and golden, that seemed hardened by my presence, and stood before me, now and then even taller than myself, with a kind of obvious surrender and prayer. As if they wished me to carry them elsewhere, indeed to some mysterious

Elsewhere with a capital E, where things would be as
we desired them in our simpler heart that endures all the
sophistications of society, where they would with due
worship undo my buttons, so trim with ivory, and unlace
my boots, so black and bright with Nathaniel's care, and
find beneath all these fine things a body as crisp as an
angel, the skin as white as last fires, the sex as fierce and
gentle as a philosophy that would undo and explain the
meaning of the world in one moment. The sex as rare as
some tight metal from the deepest earth, that would
somehow impale them and be impaled in one moment.
And in that queer moment of ravishment I would destroy
their social natures so that they issued forth into the
imperial streets at dusk redeemed and at last elevated
beyond the strictures of sin. All these matters I read in
those drawn faces, women who would soon wither so
cruelly in those ironical suns, and without a doubt die
before their time and lie in the English bone-yards so
plentifully supplied. Christ of their desires I could never
be, yet in those hours where I danced and talked and
regarded their cold passionate faces, there was a sort
of lonely marriage, separation and death, repeated ad
finitum as long as youth was mine.

*A moment, dirtied stream of music. Miss Nightingale
looks amazed by these confessions. She gathers
herself.*

Miss Nightingale Well, if you are quite finished, strange
Mr Witherchops, strange, startling Mr Witherchops,
I will finish *my* story – Yes, it was in that waiting time,
before we were allowed our way, and I could start to
spend the thirty thousand pounds of monies I had been
able to raise and gather and bring with me, and send my
own man into Constantinople where he, far beyond the
frozen powers of the army itself, was able to find
thousands of items of clothing for the men, for half of

them lay in their beds quite naked to the day, and
blankets, and all the necessities of mere breathing life –
well, it was in that waiting time, that absurd, bizarre and
unwonted time, that one day I was crossing the great
inner court of the hospital, the sun teeming on my head,
and I was stopped in my progress by an officer on a high
black horse. Or at least it seemed high, because the man
himself had fully the figure of a dwarf, or a strange
reduced figure in a fairy tale, a sort of miniature personage
that even a circus would not scorn to advertise, not
unlike – (*indicating Dr Barry*) – but, well, I will not
insult you. And this was a person of obvious rank, not
one of the doctors as I discovered later in charge at
Scutari, but someone visiting the sites of disaster as the
idle do in a time of furlough. His eyes found me with the
hunger of a merciless hawk, and his high squeaking
tones bid me quite brutally to halt, and he launched
himself into a vile tirade of abuse, something about the
nature of my dress, the fact that my head was bare and
unprotected from the sun, that I wore no jacket or coat,
that I was a disgrace and a defamation to the place.
Perhaps at first he thought I was one of those low
nurses, but soon he was adding my name into the abuse,
as if he was full of the borrowed fright and loathing of
his fellow doctors, to see the vision of a meddling
woman brought out to correct their horrible regimes at
the behest of the British parliament, and could not but
delight in discharging his hate and his distaste. Never
in my life had I met such a hardened person, even in
the army, and I stood in the beating sunlight and gazed
up at him, truly as if he were so odd and unexpected an
apparition that we did not share the same sphere on this
earth. I am sure he was one of those evilly ignorant men
who, by their customs and practices had brought the
army of England to this awful pass. He looked like a
very demon, a mere creature, and was shrivelled and

45

shrunken in his rather gorgeous uniform, his pitiless, spite-haggard features as sharp as blades, his skin white as a peeled apple under the sharp two-sided hat. Grotesque, ill-mannered, or worse quite mannerless, low-born and bizarre, dressed up as a gentleman the way an actor of no ability might be, far too spick and evilly span, with collar cutting into his hen's neck like two white knives, as if he was committing suicide with his shirt, and those little anger-tight patent shoes, all daggerlike too and dolefully shining, and running behind his high pinched horse, a little black dog with hair seemingly growing out of its very eyeballs, barking in hysteria, and a dejected African serving man trotting after like a shadow, and a goat, which to his credit I believe he brought with him to benefit from the good qualities of its milk. I was told afterwards, when he died at length some . . . some sixty years ago, that this indescribable person was actually in origin a woman. What do you think of that?

A moment, a few moments. Their faces looking out.

Dr Barry Memory turns upon small points. Of course I am as old as the Cork hills of my childhood. Two things like the two sides of a sixpence: on one side the face of Napoleon. In his last days on St Helena, I was recommended to him as a fine young doctor, and was readying myself for the voyage to him. It excited me greatly in prospect to attend such a flame of Europe's history, though time and her ironies had dampened down that fire. It moved me to think that a person so great, albeit the enemy of England so long and so grievous, might now languish in sickness and dread of death on that island where nothing, not even history, happened. But before I could set out, the dark news of his death reached me. My effects were unpacked again with a philosophical regret.

Miss Nightingale That is very remarkable.

A moment.

I begin to be anxious about the great silence of this
place. There is a lack of anyone attending us, no? I think
it would be an ease of the mind if you would speak to
me. What times is it?

*She looks at the clock, takes in the fact that it hasn't
progressed. She takes out her watch again in alarm
and looks at it. She shakes it, puts it to her ear.*

They still agree, clock and watch, but they have neither
crawled on an iota.

She is almost tearful.

I grow afraid, and I am not suited to it. What time will
the trains run to if this great clock is stopped? When the
trains no longer run on time, then we may say English
life is over. Is there not a little bell to ring for someone
to come? I see nothing. Can you not help me?

She looks towards the outside. A moment.

I do not feel as brave as you, to be looking out there.

She fetches out her Bible hurriedly.

So I will find solace in this old book, Mr Witherchops.
If you don't mind.

She opens her little Bible and reads in it.

Ah, here, should it interest you, is a photograph of
myself with Sir Harry. He tricked me into it, the subtle
fellow that he was. For I feared such a theft of soul
and heart as this. (*Shows the photograph in Dr Barry's
direction. No response.*) I look quite hideous. How he
did ever love me I do not know. He carried it with him
his whole life, it seems, and when he died it arrived from

47

his lawyer in an official envelope, and although I felt it almost as a reproach, I was thankful to have it, as a memorial of his nice face.

Dr Barry On the other face of that little sixpence peers out the features of that supposed reformer, Florence Nightingale.

Miss Nightingale glances up.

She did no more than I had been doing for thirty years, and that without changing out of her skirts. At the height of the Crimean War, her criticisms of the army hospitals there brought me to inspect them. I felt bound to defend things as they were, which was not my wont. I could not sing her song. Perhaps I was wrong. But something about her enraged me, what I cannot say. One day crossing the parade ground on my black stallion, I spied a self-important woman crossing in the close midday heat, with only a scrap of a bonnet on her head. All about milled the dark soldiery. I knew that it was her. Something unpleasant and inexplicable seized me. I began to berate her, fixing her there before all those rough hearts and souls, crying down at her for risking that deluge of sun and heat, against the clear regulations. Moving about a male place as if she had the God-given right to move there, independent and austere. Maybe as she looked up at me she thought me a hardened savage, a mere puff of military stricture on a horse more sensible than its rider. I gave her the blackguarding of her life and kicked my horse onward. I do not know what possessed me, except it was rage so sore and wild and resentful it near stopped my old throat like a collapsing mine. She had not had to change out of her skirts to be the personage she was, and she was young then still, and used her pretty face to get her way with drains and bandages.

Miss Nightingale has risen to her feet, her arm raised.

Miss Nightingale You, you, it is you! All this time,
listening to you! Rapscallion! You Irish blackguard!
What horror is this that I find myself here at the edge
of perdition, for all I know, in this lonely room, in these
realms of loneliness where great engines converge,
coming up out of Gloucester and down from the Lakes,
seeing from their windows quite different country,
meeting at last at the station, the spread of yards and
sidings like wings, like an angel fallen to the earth, that
I, a notable personage, should be cloistered by this
garrulous, opinionated, seditious midget!

A moment, Dr Barry heaped in his sorrows.

And yet, and yet, I know his story now. Not just the
ditch of rumour and gossip, which after all I have often
decried. The strange uncle, the books, the tragic mother.
Well, I wish, I demand of myself to be enraged by you,
to discipline you, to bring you to heel, you Irish mongrel.
But . . . Humanity . . . Truth . . . A solitary soul, a lonely
heart.

A moment.

But are you not dead these many, many years? And when
you died, was your name not mired in a filthy story?

*Dr Barry rises stiffly and goes to the door. Light there
turning.*

Dr Barry I am nothing, it is true. A filth, a darkness.
My own history hurts me. It is all despicable, horrible.
No God could consider me, or to His heaven admit me.

A moment.

It is true I was the lover of the governor, but it is hard for
me to describe the nature and pattern of that love. The

49

governor was one of those familied men who nevertheless have an ardent and indeed verdant impulse towards other men. He sought to possess me as a kind of miniature man, a slight thing who nevertheless showed a force and authority in that world, a contradictory person of both balsa wood and iron.

Miss Nightingale Well, I am glad now you would not address me. You are an affront to any kind of company.

Dr Barry He was a man of entirely noble birth, and while infected with many of the lassitudes of his class and position, pursued his other need with urgency and success. For myself I will say his face was a welcome star and his form an intoxicating suggestion of delight. You hate me now?

Miss Nightingale Hate? If I were a magistrate, I would imprison you, like one of those lusting aesthetes, to sew mail sacks, to break stones for your sins!

Dr Barry It was a dark night of that far African place, when I attended him in the luxury of candlelight in his encushioned rooms, for some concocted complaint, that he put his arms about me, and kissed my unkissed mouth.

Miss Nightingale Oh, please, please do not recount these foul matters, keep them to yourself. Please!

Dr Barry All the bitterness of my life, the constraint, the secrecy and the harm, fled away, and I stood up against his greater self like a long dog, a sweet lion, and took his kiss with gratitude. He put me on his bed and fumbled his member towards me, and I naturally opened my flies and took him to me. Perhaps he was astonished to find his member sink down into some soft hot place, but he did not betray that surprise, but caressed me and pulsed his seed into me. Then I put order again on my clothes and he got back into his regal bed and I ministered to his supposed ailment. We did not speak a word. Then, trembling and half-entranced, I walked out into the pungent darkness, walking home between the high walls of those imperial gardens, happy as I had never been nor was again. Three times more I lay with the governor, him expressing nothing but joy, always hurried and half-brutal, half-gentle, like a man seems to be. Then in the town appeared a foul notice, a sort of authorless libel, that called me the little wife of the governor, and raised a dampened-down furore of gossip and scandal in the city. For weeks I went out about my official affairs with a dread of the world, yet forcing myself to keep a severe face and say nothing. Of course my connection and love was broken, and never again did we lie together, the governor and myself. And yet I will say it was a pure and absolute love, though indeed he was wed, it was a strange love without English or history, existing instead in a realm of story and dream. Of course I must relate with a hard mercilessness towards my own soul that some months later I was horrified to identify in myself a pregnancy, and saw swelling on my slim belly the unmistakable sign, and at length felt tiny elbows and knees as I thought dancing out against my skin. I took myself away on leave to a close island, with only Nathaniel and Psyche, intending to bear the child and have it somehow cared for by other persons, but truly I had no good plan. By a ferocious irony my little one was born dead, in a terrible night of pain and muddle, my good Nathaniel as tender and strong as any midwife, labouring in the shame and mystery of his master.

Against her will, Miss Nightingale is moved.

I think he thought I was a demon of another earth, a creature from the stories of his childhood in the Hibernian realm of Jamaica, but because he loved me as a servant, he did what was asked of him, without question or reproach. The little chap was born dead, I listened for his heartbeat myself in the languor of that final exhaustion. I wept as a mother for the loss and Nathaniel in silence wrapped the little corpse in fresh linens, and bore him down to the margins of the sea, and assigned him to the warm African waters, in mercy, secrecy and love. The milk that came and hurt my breast seemed also to assail my very heart, and I wept in my darkness, and I wept.

Miss Nightingale (*after a little, simply*) I nearly understand you.

A moment.

I would not marry Sir Harry, I could not in truth, because of desolations that seemed to stretch like impassable lands before me, I could not embrace him, I could not lie, one to one, like those knights and their ladies on the ancient tombs, my feet could not go forward to that, it was as if I were an inhabitant of some Italian town all heavy with its saints and churches, and some great fall of snow had come down in the night, and now as I travelled the roads my boots could get no grip, and the lights of the candled town shone down across the gripped plain and mocked me, and I was not able to be a woman in that guise, but a soldier of medicine certainly, a woman that could climb the Matterhorn on a Sunday, but not be a visitor to the bosky hills of human love.

A moment.

Poor Harry in his grief said I should have been born a man, because I was like a man and worse than a man, in my ambitions.

Miss Nightingale rises and peers at a print of an Egyptian pyramid on the wall. She touches it.

You have stirred my head in mysterious ways, my dear Mr Witherchops, if I may still call you that. I did my great deed at Scutari, but was a person alone. Childless, without Harry, and alone. A woman should not need the confirmation, affirmation, of a mere marriage. Nor the bloody wars of childbirth.

A moment.

And yet such hardship of soul it brought me. In all honesty, to confess that fact . . . The confusion almost unto madness. Apostasy! My dear Mr Witherchops, you are in the halfpenny place there. I was that reckless woman who spent twenty years inventing her own religion! To give it to the working people of England, that was my thought. To reform the army hospitals, yes, and then to cry out to the very heavens, and invent a remedy for all English souls. What really moved me I hardly know. My body just a curtain of rotted cloth. My heart a crumbling wafer. Oh, Mr Witherchops, whoever and whatever you are, we are not so entirely unlike.

A moment.

And some time later I sat in the temple of Karnak and felt the dance of my life was done. I did not say it to myself, I felt it as an essence both evil and good seeping through the walls of myself. It is by far the ugliest building in the ancient world that I have seen, its huge and silly columns ponderously rising, its blunt unchristian tones. But I liked it, surprised myself by liking it. It had no purpose now but to excite fat tourists expensively suffering the pagan echoes and the dysenteries of Egypt. So it was rather apt in a roundabout way. I was alone, it was the edge of evening, when travellers return to their gilded lairs. The guides had brought them back with their smiling, mirthless faces. All noises were gone, and only the sunlight remained, dazed and ragged between the massive stones. A small bird, stripped these centuries

of his sacred attribute, stabbed at the remnants of
poisonous picnics. I was alone with the bird, the rearing
temple, and the vanished purpose. I gathered my skirts
against my skin, and a sudden feeling of worthlessness
and strange disaster filled me. What was to come after
what had been, after transforming that screaming
hospital in Scutari in sixteen weeks into a relative haven
of cleanliness and good drains? The heroic mathematics
that had been gathering around my life, had twisted and
turned, its numbers tumbling in the ether, and had
offered an equitable result. I was grateful for that of
course. But not so deep in that mathematics had been a
self-tormenting voice quite silenced by action, a horrible
understanding of my own evil that had torn at all solace
and peace of mind. Now I feared, without the obstacle
of some great future effort, some other Scutari that
would rescue me, I would be returned to the suffering.
I was so horrified at the prospect my brow began to
sweat, and then my arms and legs, my back seeped into
my clothes like blood, I was drenched by terror. The bird
flew up. Now standing in its place was a golden man,
with brow as clear as a child's, his large hands stretched
out towards me, dressed in a gown with the blue of
shells. Around him in that moment bloomed a sudden
light like the strange explosion of a photograph. It seemed
to me in my fear and sudden love that he was asking me
to do his work, without that hope of reputation. He
didn't speak, of course, he looked at me with those
unfearing eyes, the kindest eyes I ever saw, and the sickles
of light in those eyes were like two ancient moons. Long
drawn planes of light made his face as if perpetually
moving, his beauty so keen and dry passing through me
like a regiment of modest prayers. This was not like that
time when I was a girl of seventeen, when I heard the
voice of God, also asking me to do his work. This was
a vision of clear reality. Here was the figure of all our

lives, our explicator, the emperor of souls, slain by his
own people, the purposeful man. I whispered to myself,
he exists, he existed, it is all plain and true, there is
a purpose in the world beyond the great turning and
turning of the generations, the seed of man ploughed
back, and man springing forth again, those circles and
cycles I had stood out of, as if balanced on the rim of
nothing. The Book of Life seemed after all to contain my
pitiful name, I would look down at length at close of day
and read it there before I passed for good or ill into the
bleak eternity of waiting. Such peace overwhelmed me
in that silly pagan place. And yet he had chosen well.
Suddenly that strange temple seemed lovely too, framing
his gentle limbs, transformed his holiness and perfection
into an architectural prayer. I could not move, I could not
speak, it seemed like freaks of silver light were streaming
from my eyes. The lights coiled and gathered around him.
Something terrific and awful occurred beyond my
knowledge and understanding. We were not betrothed,
not wedded, but some great idea was present, so that it
seemed all of Egypt echoed with its wordless meanings.
The darkening monuments with their moaning ruins.
The long speckled bird that now returned. The sky
glistening with flung fragments of lost colour. The dying
earth in the gathering night.

*She comes down quite close to Dr Barry. They stand
almost hand to hand.*

Dr Barry (*in pain*) This is my body now, that has caused
me such an adventure of evasion and aloneness. It was
my hope that in my last days at least there would be a
perfect secrecy, a silence as of death, but maybe attended
by some latter ease. There was none of that. My heart
fulminated against my fate, my memory brooded on the
wrongs done against me, the preferment withheld, the
lack of signs from my sovereign that I had served these

kingdoms well in the strange gardens of the Empire. It
may be that I did not. My vanity seemed to tell me that,
by railing against the mires and boglands of things as
they were, I was bringing new lustre to the story of these
islands. Perhaps it was not so. For the hearts of kings
and queens, if cold and queer, at least are grateful. And
I was not shown gratitude. I linger because I cannot
leave while my only legacy is whispered spite and scandal.
I wish I were a person in an age when my achievements
might be seen as mighty things, that would not reduce
my remnant life to a miserable scurry of rumour and
disgust. Even last night as I lay dead – or perhaps it only
seems like last night, and this limbo has the timeless time
of hell, perhaps it was a week, a year, or fifty years – the
dirty Irish nurse from down the street came in to lay me
out, stripping the nightdress from my morbid limbs,
her breath no doubt if I could have smelt it inflammable
with alcohol. A stray light would have sent flames issuing
forth from her ancient mouth like a veritable dragon.
For fifty years no one had seen me put on my clothes,
much less take them off, not even a Nathaniel. Only a
Psyche had seen such hard matters. Oh dull, white nightdress given to man to wear! What was I to her, only a
dead doctor of no repute, a mere streak of Englishman
in an austere lodging in the endless city of London. It
was as if my fate decreed that it would be one of my
own countrymen, or countrywomen, who would pick
over my lifeless bones, and rub them down with a
grubby cloth, and reach down to plug my poor orifices
against the foul leaks of death. Oh how she did murmur
and even delight to find me out, to finger the blue
stretch-marks on my old belly, to spy out that little
lonesome cleft that gave her such surprise. How smugly
she informed my lovely doctor, a man of such discretion
he never touched my person with finger or instrument,
and who was my deepest friend in my last extremity.

And she asked for money to keep my secret and he gave
her some silver coins. They did not stay her mouth. And
so my story is reduced to this, a drunken old woman
fumbling in the parts of a helpless, dead personage, and
anything I did to redress the unforgivable imbalances
of this pretty world is as nothing, swallowed up in the
Leviathan of this revelation. And so, though I long to
go, I cannot go, for there is no approbation, no love
of monarch or mortal, to release me. Here I abide as
the mourner of myself, as the rememberer of my own
heart, waiting in this waiting room, even the desperate
celebrator of an imprisoned soul. I would knock upon
the earth and cry, like Chaucer's old pilgrim man, *Lovely
mother, let me in* – but she cannot take me, she will not
take me, with so much cruel history blowing round my
ruined head.

*Psyche barking, but her barking fading away. Hooting
of the little owl now.*

Miss Nightingale Athena? Calling again in this living
world?

A moment.

No, of course not, not in this living world. Of course,
I see what it is – I am dead also. If this lost personage is
dead, then I must be too – and no doubt just as lost, into
the bargain. In the small hours, extinguished at last, like
a speck of ash in the cold grate. The end of life, of all
love . . . No matter. I think I knew it from the start, but
I could not bring myself entirely to say it. I have slipped
away from my little bed like a spectre. Well, well, I cannot
mourn myself. Let the leaf blow from the great tree.
Victoria herself grew old, her divinity was assailed, old
Father Death folded her in his coats and drew her away.
Was I not soon to follow? Of course. Having outlived
my friends, every one, I seem now to have outlived

myself. There is more *life* in me, here, than there has been for many a recent yesterday. (*looking in the mirror*) There is even a suggestion –

She glances about for somewhere to put the music box, finds nowhere, and hands it to Dr Barry, who holds it without comment.

– of veritable youthfulness, (*tending her hair a moment*) which is unobjectionable. To creep up on your ninetieth year is a creeping only, we the old are the babies without futures, we are the tragic bairns, as the Scottish soldiers used to say, of the shadowing world. We slip away into that nameless place where science, philosophy, religion and art have never convincingly penetrated. It is the realm of spirit, I suppose, or of nothing, and if the spirit we may hope and pray some majesty of the breathing earth still maintains, some noble collaboration of verdant hills, with seams of rills sounding throughout, and the company of whoever may have passed the rigorous gates of that putative St Peter. Will Dante speak to me in tongues, Lucretius expound the rainbow and the owl, will those noble friends of my days, Sidney Herbert, who nobly slaved to fulfil for me the behest of my visionary Christ, take my hand again, great Benjamin Jowett explain again Plato's chariot of the soul, the horse of reason pulling against the horse of instinct, or Sir Harry Verney trick me into being photographed a second time by the celestial camera of souls that will show our true contour and our inner worth? I pray they might. I do not know why I have been sent to this place to hear out this ruined creature, who is so lost, so mired in himself, or herself, she cannot hear me. How long must she linger? Or myself? And, it strikes me, to annotate that thought, has she been waiting all these sixty years, for someone like me, who disdained her, to hear her heart? Or is it the weight of sins that keeps us both, or was one

needed to free the other? I would gladly let her go. If by
my will, my understanding, my listening, I might do it.
Then will the voice of my God issue forth from a divine
face made visible at last? And will I wonder in the halls
of God, and know some hidden things, my heart sing
with the plenty of the blessed, and my memory feel only
the echoing remnants of my mortality, and wonder
therefore how goes it with the world of living beings,
how satiate with wars, how pressing on for peace? I do
not know, of course. Into the fiery pit I may be thrown
myself, for my petulance, my impropriety, and my faith.
God may have the sanction of a father. He alone must
judge. If to the fiery pit I must descend, may he grant me
a moment to glimpse His face, and to think again on all
that I have seen, and understand before the closing of the
doors the purpose of our journeys and the meaning of
our prayers.

*A moment. The two. Dr Barry opens the music-box.
The music.*

Dr Barry Despite official resistance to my reforming
nature, I must allow I reached high rank in my progress
through that imperial army. Inspector General of Army
Hospitals. How the spirit of General Miranda must
smile, to witness from the halls of death the triumph
of his thirteen-year-old protégée. Not just a woman, but
an Irish woman, not just as Irishwoman, but a Catholic
to boot. How easily I entered that supposed male world
of difficulty and challenge, and brought recalcitrant
officialdom to heel, and played my part. But in the upshot,
I must confess, it seems a hollow victory. Perfection
is not contained in fine careers, alas, but in the quality
of love a pilgrim soul may show. And high quality of
human love is rare. And indeed no matter what we say
and show, no matter even if love is gained or given, all
things pass away, histories, sparrows, importances and

countries, empires and the knots and miniatures of families. The clocks disprove us all, and even we, immortal in our chosen clothes, will pass in a moment of gentle or violent grief from the realm of ordinary to-ing and fro-ing, to a final completeness of darkness. We will be remembered for better or ill until even our rememberers follow us into that same and utter blankness. Our shirts and socks, our umbrellas, our snuffboxes and our combs, will scatter after us like things in an explosion. Crack of floor will take the comb, some future wind will blow out the brolly, and it will be thrown like a ruined blackbird into the welcoming midden. We will lie in the earth as snug and forgotten as the mummified mice under the hearthstone. It is God's mercy. Time will close over our passage, the little eddy we made across the pond of daily life, until it will be as if we had never lived. This is why no one creature, no emperor or pauper, has an especial importance. This is why humanity itself is but a laughable storm of leaves and ash. This is why every man's story is the whisper of God. This is why we are redeemed at last, because nothing else can be done for us. Worn out, erased, breathless and disdained by the merriments of tomorrow, we will cry out for forgiveness and be forgiven, for God takes each and every one and makes him new, returns him to the crisp clear lines of the original mould, relieves him of his heavy sins, and in His wise mercy lets him go into that strange eternity where there is no earthly story and no human song. To that mercy now my heart calls out. I pray, I pray for that.

Miss Nightingale (*quietly*) If I can intercede, you shall have it. I will bombard the government of Heaven, assault the ministries of angels, on your behalf. It will be my task.

Leak of dawnlight from above, like a sacred painting. Light from behind binds them. The fringes of decrepitude displacing the waiting room, framing them. A whole music, a rescuing music. There is the quality of a daguerreotype about them – a strange marriage, an unexpected couple. The owl calling softly. Their nearest hands just touching, perhaps by accident. And the dark retrieves them.

Finis.

FRED AND JANE

Fred and Jane was first produced at the Bewley's Café Theatre, Dublin, in August 2002. The cast was as follows:

Anna Nagle Mary McEvoy
Beatrice Dunne Lette Proctor

Directed by Caroline Fitzgerald
Designed by Emma Cullen
Lighting by Moyra Darcy
Produced by Kelly Campbell

Characters

Beatrice
Anna

*The ante-room of a convent. Slow milling of sunlight.
Rich polish of wood. Sense of care.*

*Two nuns seated, Anna about thirty, Beatrice in her
sixties, vigorous, bony. Expectant, like horses before the
off. They are being interviewed, the questions as if edited
out.*

Beatrice (*Midlands accent*) No assumptions, that would
be the main thing.

Anna (*middle-class Dublin accent*) Yes. I'd agree with
that. No assumptions. We'll just go from the start for
you. But if you thought you knew about it already . . .
For our part, we'll be as candid as possible, as open as
we can, after all these years of relative . . .

Beatrice A good layer and a bad hen are often found in
the one bird.

Anna There's a proper country background for you.
I wish I had that!

Beatrice A good layer and a bad hen . . . She'll give eggs,
but she'll hide them. If you want to find them, you've to
learn to think like her. And under old tractor parts you'll
get them, old traps that were pushed aside in the fifties
for the motor car.

Anna I think I especially was drawn to her because she
was from the Midlands.

Beatrice Lord, don't mention the Midlands.

Anna She thinks there's no respect for the Midlands in Dublin. We have a joke about that.

Beatrice The whole country has a joke about that. Unless you're from the Midlands, you know.

Anna But Meath was the centre of Ireland once. The Midlands were once considered the sacred part of Ireland.

Beatrice Dublin's revenge on Tara – Mullingar heifers. A phrase to terrorise you.

Anna As you can see, she's no heifer.

Beatrice Well, now. I've seen some pretty heifers in my day. I've seen heifers would put Lauren Bacall in the penny place. My own father had heifers he doted on. We used to worry about that. My mother and me, in the kitchen.

Anna Usually in a Dublin family you'll find a farm somewhere. But not in ours. Before Finglas was built up, my great-grandmother . . . But aside from that. And of course now . . .

Beatrice That's the why we wouldn't want assumptions. Because it's generally believed among the people that nuns like guards are country people. But Anna, as you can see plainly . . .

Anna People think also that country families love their daughters to go off being nuns.

Beatrice Oh, God. If only!

Anna She had a mighty struggle, a mighty struggle. She says she had to bribe her father . . . Tell her, Beatrice.

Beatrice Oh – well, it wasn't just only the heifers. I'm afraid, just between ourselves, and Lord love him, he's

dead now, of course, and I hope for his sake he managed
to . . . square things with Father O'Malley . . . What a
man he was for the scarves. Oh, dear. Was it Mullingar
or Gomorrah, you are thinking now. But yes, I believe in
a fair picture of things, but there were things I knew
about him, I'd seen him at the edges of the darkness, you
know, those little spaces in the country after dark, when
light from somewhere unexpectedly . . . That's when you
see the secrets.

Anna He was handsome like Beatrice.

Beatrice Handsome? I suppose he must have been. Or
they thought so. Various shop girls, nothing too
ambitious!

Anna She had the dope on him.

Beatrice Aye – and when I got the yen . . . To tell you
the truth – I could go into that later, in a minute. You
see, I had a sort of vision. (*After a moment.*) Yes.

Anna A vision, she had. A real one. Like Saint What-
Are-You-Having in Lourdes. Bernadette.

Beatrice Oh, I was fourteen. There wasn't a boy would
go out with Beatrice Dunne because she was as tall as a
dray horse. Well, to them. They were only little boys that
time. That's all that was going those days, with the diet.
Well, I was keen for a boyfriend and the pictures. I could
have made decent use of one. Not a bit of it. The devil
wouldn't play. So one Saturday I asked my mother for a
penny or tuppence or whatever was the asking price, and
I went off to town and the pictures on my own – like a
gangster!

Anna There's style for you.

Beatrice This would be the thirties, you see. Fred and
Ginger were all the talk then. The couples in those

primitive times modelled themselves on Fred and Ginger. Well, we were all there, the youth of Mullingar and outlying districts – huffing and puffing at each other they were. I felt like a lamb among wolves. I was that envious, that kissing going on, that wonderful rich noisy kissing Mullingar couples perfected at that time. Because it didn't do just to press the lips together. It was quite complex, you know, there were styles of arm-wrestling . . .

Anna Isn't she great?

Beatrice But the bit I don't think they saw was when Fred and Ginger were dancing and . . . A balcony, and that white light and the white floor . . . Fine music someone had got up for them . . . Oh, and I saw a dove came down from the top of the picture and sit on Fred Astaire's head . . .

Anna The Holy Ghost it was called then.

Beatrice Aye, aye, the Holy Ghost, Lord love us. I was sitting there. Fred paid no heed to it. Didn't mind one way or the other. Kissing went on. But for myself . . . Decisive. So I blackmailed my father to let me go to . . . to the cats, he called it. He had his wits about him. Lord, he was angry though. Fuming. But he was a bit stymied, because of the dope I had on him, as Anna says.

Anna They might have made a fair go of it, with pilgrims and such like, in Mullingar, out of Beatrice's vision.

Beatrice But you couldn't make a shrine out of the Capital Cinema, girl, the people wouldn't like it.

Anna But wasn't Ballinspittle a garage?

Beatrice I didn't hear that. Was it? Oh, but where would the couples have gone then? The last thing they'd want is some spotty girl getting the cinema dismantled, and holy terrors milling around after miracles . . . It was a private vision. My own.

Anna Of course it was. I was joking with you. I'm ashamed to have joked with you, Beatrice.

Beatrice Of course you're not ashamed. Why shouldn't you joke? It was a ridiculous vision. Fred Astaire, I ask you. But it suited me at the time. I was glad it wasn't that dreadful Caesar Romero, with the grease he used to put in his hair.

Anna She had the cream of the cinema at her beck and call.

Beatrice I used to wake up when I was a novice in the middle of the night and see Fred standing in the corner of the room, smiling very nicely. I must say he did always smile very nicely. At the back of my mind I wanted Gary Cooper to turn up, just the once, for the effect. Or Henry Fonda. Do you remember the time Ingrid Bergman left her husband and went off with the Italian director? Hollywood was very annoyed with her. Hollywood! Gomorrah itself. I was delighted for her. Because, I think my father imagined he was married to me, in a manner of speaking. Oh, how he went on. He used to drool when he was angry, because his head tilted forward and all the juice ran out down his chins. Hmm. I ran off anyhow, to the great Italian Director in the sky!

Anna Beatrice!

Beatrice Oh, well. You're not shocked, are you? Not a bit of it.

Anna She's neither sense nor discretion betimes.

Beatrice I have plenty of both, thank you very much. You're a one to rebuke me, that fancied yourself as Jane Fonda in *Klute*, as you're always saying, and were intent on being an actress. A fine example. A prostitute, no less. In the film, I mean. Oh, yes, I've had to sit through it a number of times. I've nothing against prostitutes as a matter of fact, but I can't let her away with that, that self-righteous . . .

Anna She was fantastic in *Klute*. Imagine seeing that at fifteen. I was with my brother. He was nineteen and got me in as his girlfriend. That was it. Flash of understanding. Jane Fondahood. Acting.

Beatrice She could have been an actress. She has the figure and the voice.

Anna Jane Fonda, I worshipped you. I have the tape. The fitness tape? She's fifty or something like it. Fifty!

Beatrice Thank you.

Anna Sorry, Beatrice. Fifty, and fit and shapely as a fiddle, I meant.

Beatrice Her father Henry never put on weight. I doubt if he danced about like that. In the blood.

Anna I'd have killed to be an actress. Wanting to be an actress at that age – a disease. A fire. you sit in the fire, not burning up. But burning.

Beatrice You still hanker after it. She still hankers after it, believe me, the poor girl. And she has the face and the figure and the voice still. Maybe we should encourage her to try her luck.

Anna I see. Now you can do without me all of a sudden.

Beatrice I'll come with you and be your dresser. I can be that splendid black actress, what was her name? Used to play the dresser in all the films. Like that chap lives in Ireland used to play all the bellhops and the desk clerks, Hoagy Carmichael.

Anna O. Z. Whitehead, Beatrice.

Beatrice Yes, him. Dublin naturally is and was the haunt of famous actors. Did you know that all the stars I've mentioned visited Dublin down the years? And where was I? In a nunnery in the Midlands. Coming to Dublin was the making of me, though I missed the stars I was interested in. Fred was here a few years back, but not the same Fred. He looked like a survivor. A man who had survived being Fred Astaire. I mean, he looked grand. But not for visiting out in Collinstown.

Anna Dublin Airport.

Beatrice Whatever they call it now. I was there the one time in the fifties. They had little tables out on the tarmac where you could have tea or, would you believe, coffee, and the planes were fat and silver. It was when the Bishop of – of – well, he was coming back from Africa. We were all there, all the dames in black, waving. It wasn't the same as a film star, as you can imagine. A Wicklow man, the bishop, Dunne by name. No relation. He was said to be avuncular. He didn't get a chance to avunculate me, though. Too lowly, I must have been. Back to the Midlands that night, on the train. The lot of us exhausted. Girls we were. Ignorant, but full of life and speculation. But not like Anna when I met her.

Anna You rogue. Not like Anna. Really.

Beatrice Anna Nagle, will I ever forget her, seventeen years old, a streak of misery.

Anna Oh, well!

Beatrice But very nice, you were lovely. A Monkstown girl. Lovely. Everyone admired you for taking the plunge, in an era when plunges weren't often taken, plunges of that sort.

75

Anna My acting career . . .

Beatrice My vision . . .

They laugh.

Aren't we the ones, with our carry-on? (*After a bit.*) Of
course, you had boyfriends, galore. Before . . .

Anna A flood. When my mother would be going out,
you know, to the theatre or whatever, in the evening, she
used to say, 'Après moi, le déluge.'

Beatrice Louis the Fourteenth. Oh, you know . . .

Anna And sure enough, in they'd come, Simon and
Gerry and the rest, and they'd drink her Bacardi. She
hated Bacardi, so there was usually a bottle. You had to
have it for – some drink grown-ups used to drink then.
The fashion. The poor old deluge. Where are they now?
They were good types. Then we'd hear her coming home,
and away off out the back into the garden with them
and over the back wall and into the old field. She didn't
mind them in the house because she trusted me and she
liked the deluge. But it was a point of honour with them
not to be caught and identified by 'the conspiracy', as
they called the parents. I was almost entirely Jane Fonda
by then, and would sit in the armchair looking like I'd
just had a pretty demanding evening. All we did really
was drink tiny amounts of Bacardi and play don – do
you know that game?

Beatrice My sinful Anna!

Anna Well, you see, I was very keen to be a nun the
summer after that, but I was ferociously sad to lose the
deluge. And that was why I was a streak of misery when
Beatrice found me. The others thought I was a pious
snob, but I was just missing the deluge. Then Beatrice,
as you will have gathered, was obviously a sort of deluge

rolled into one. A mate. So I cheered up. I got into gear. She put flowers an the altar of little Anna Nagle. Bingo.

Beatrice I don't know why she refers to a dignified old woman like me as a flood. The day the Pope landed on Phoenix Park I thought I was going to have to beat her, drive her back over the rugby grounds to Parkgate Street. She was like a puppy that won't obey the simplest commands. I had to hold on to her cord. She kept hugging me and then bolting away nearer to the cross, and all sorts of esteemed religious bumped in the process.

Anna All right for you, nine feet tall. I wanted to see him properly. A man like that. He gave up a career in the theatre to be Pope.

Beatrice Well, the sacrifice. And not exactly, Anna.

Anna To be a priest. And do you know, he was the spit of Jane Fonda. Or Peter, anyway.

Beatrice He's not the slightest bit like any of the Fondas. Such a thing to say about the Holy Father. My God, Anna, but you see what you want to see. You always did . . . (*After a bit.*) Jimmy Cagney I might allow . . .

Anna That old gangster? I'm sure the Pope would much rather be compared to Peter Fonda than Jimmy Cragface Cagney.

Beatrice Cagney looked just fine when he was young. He played Shakespeare, on celluloid. *Midsummer Night's Dream*. Beautiful diction.

Anna And what part did he play, Beatrice?

Beatrice Bottom.

Anna See? Bottom. Jimmy Cagney. The Pope.

Beatrice It was just after that that the trouble started.

Anna Yes, it was. I still don't know why they decided . . . They didn't care what we felt . . . They didn't even know we . . . It's like the Civil Service in here betimes. Words from on high. We must obey. The Earthlings will do as follows. The Daleks.

Beatrice After my time.

Anna Bureaucracy for nuns.

Beatrice We considered . . . various options . . .

Anna Well, we sat back that day, we heard and we wept like kids.

Beatrice You do feel powerless. Quite the same sensation when my father died. Or when they told me he was, you know, dead. Apoplexy. It seemed to me an old-fashioned thing to die of, but apparently you still can – die of it, I mean. Apoplexy. A man that never let a day go by without practising for it.

Anna My father's still alive but he's stuffed into one of those homes. Run by nuns, of course. Too many years without my mother. Never a successful pairing. Anyway, he had anal cancer and they took it out in Monkstown Hospital. I don't know if my mother went to see him. He used to read old letters to me that he saw on the napkins, or thought he did. Hard drugs! Then he came back from that but he fell down the metal stairs of a 46A bus – the common bus, we used to call it, because it went through Monkstown Farm. The 8 went very sweetly by the sea road. Old nonsense. The conductor caught him, but he banged his old head. He's happier now than he's been for years, with his little room and Tennyson and Kipling for company. Not dogs, the real thing, books. Me and Beatrice go in to see him with chocolates.

Beatrice He's my age. Which goes to show. One sandwich short of a picnic, but a splendid man. Knows reams of poems off pat. A kind of cake mixture of Tennyson and the other fellow – but captivating. The most charming man on earth.

Anna So she says. You're a charmer, Mr Nagle, she says to him. And he goes red with elegance and pleasure. Anyway, we wept like kids.

Beatrice We'd been together for fourteen years. It did frighten me, that – there was too much feeling there. Wasn't there? Too much stored up. Too many good times. That daft little girl who came in as a novice, my little actress, had flowered into a friend.

Anna At first we thought it was a punishment, because Beatrice told me there had been a sort of meeting, a tribunal, but we found out later that that's quite normal.

Beatrice They hold a tribunal for everything. If a loo breaks down they hold one. But this tribunal decided they were sending Anna to a mission in England.

Anna England. You'd think it was a land of savages. A mission to England. As if England couldn't do without Anna Nagle.

Beatrice I thought it was a bizarre decision. But of course the English cities are – this was Manchester, and that's in a right state, so Anna says.

Anna You never saw such desolation and withering of the spirit. I believe things have improved lately.

Beatrice They had you for two years, dear.

Anna We lived in a terrace house, me and two other nuns. One was a very nice woman from the Gambia. The other was a witch from Glasgow. We tried to minister to old Irish expatriates down on their luck. Was there any other sort in Manchester? Not that I saw. Good women once from Irish towns done for with drinking, and half on the street, and marrying jailbirds for the company. You might as well marry a sailor for all the company you get. Meanwhile, back at the ranch . . .

Beatrice I was here blowing sorrow up the chimney.

Anna If you read her letters today. Huge big things like sliced pans, and the best thing since. I almost ate them for news. I was very afraid.

Beatrice We knew something was up with us. It was too severe and it didn't lessen.

Anna I started to imagine I was being punished after all, and I wrote to Mother Superior in Dalkey and asked her what I'd done wrong and that I missed home dreadfully. She wrote me a lovely letter, full of surprise and tenderness. But what use was that to me, when she didn't call me back? You see, I thought maybe they imagined – no, they just considered that me and Beatrice were . . .

Beatrice Wonky. No, they do go wonky sometimes, nuns. And the boys are prone, too. The poor boys. It's a great deal worse for the boys because they're not exactly tactile at the best of times. Did you ever see a priest embrace another? They're like diplomats at airports. But nuns don't heed all that. They're sisters. If they like each other. But we began to think we'd been investigated. Someone had been looking into us. That was the madness in the business.

Anna We were so lonely without each other we imagined all sorts of things.

Beatrice Like spies must do when they hear nothing from Moscow for a few months. But it was just a straightforward mission. It's normal for our order. We kept knocking our heads on the phone over it and in my sliced-pan letters. And we never actually said the real crux of the matter. We never actually spoke the truth – we didn't know it.

Anna My whole system went out of kilter. It was like a menopause and a pregnancy rolled into one. I ate so much bad food I couldn't think for calories. My hair began to thin out – to fall out, for heaven's sake. I had more aches than a soccer player. The doctor thought I was an hysterical young nun and gave me barbiturates. I used to cry – you know those ornamental ponds? There'd be one, in the middle of my pillow. You'd be surprised how much moisture you can produce. But I was a young woman. Beatrice started to come apart like an over-boiled onion. Not that she ever told me. I thought she was doing fine, aside from mere grief.

Beatrice I did deteriorate a little.

Anna Ha. The lobster speaks. Look at me, I'm all right. Bubble, bubble, bubble. Just going a little red. Hey diddle diddle.

Beatrice I asked a little child once – he was on O'Connell Street, a Sunday. It was an All-Ireland final, in the afternoon. Meath was playing, so I went out to hear the accents! He was a skinny little fellow, seven or so, with a bag of glue. I don't usually stop. The city is so full of . . . But I did, and asked him if he was all right. You know, a foolish nun, stooping down to a little gangster. 'I'm bollixed, Mister,' he said. Mister! Still, it was a powerful expression of his situation. After a year without Anna I might have said the same. First the lining of my stomach started to ball up and then the doctor said I had ulcers. I thought elderly racing men that drank whiskey and drove across Ireland in their cars to get to meetings got ulcers. Fellows with rolls of ready bills and purple faces. But no, ordinary sixty-year-old nuns too.

Anna And she never said a mumbling word, as Odetta used to sing.

Beatrice After my time!

Anna The way I found out was, I was back for a few days – leave, to see my family. I don't even remember seeing them. All I remember is this one here, a vision of miserable – you see her now, a hale woman, a young woman . . .

Beatrice A young woman!

Anna She was like the old woman of the roads after a particularly bad winter. Thank God it's funny now, but I remember thinking, Mercy of God, she looks like an old banana in a habit.

Beatrice A charming . . .

Anna Well, you did, Beatrice.

Beatrice I had a little stomach trouble.

Anna That's right.

Beatrice Oh, I did, I looked like hell.

Anna The ghost of Fred Astaire.

Beatrice Poor Fred.

Anna If you can imagine now that we had another year and three months to go, and no guarantee I'd be brought back to Dublin at the end of that. I remember at Dunleary, those dreadful early-morning sailings, when half of the country seems to be going home to England.

Beatrice Christmas, the government's shame.

Anna And poor Beatrice among the taxis, at the iron gates. 'Look after yourself, dear,' she says, and hands me the *Independent*. Jesus Christ!

Beatrice Did you not want the *Independent*, dear?

Anna Then back to sunny Manchester. Did you ever see the bleakness of Manchester? I swear to you, a vision of revengeful hell. Old factory chimneys, old black streets, poor ashen-faced citizens. Totally and utterly without God.

Beatrice You can't say that, dear.

Anna No, I can. God is a transforming light. Totally and utterly without God.

Beatrice But, dear . . .

Anna It is possible. There was nothing for me to do there. Totally and utterly. If anyone here thought that I, Sister Anna, the wrong side of thirty, was the person to bring God to Manchester – God wouldn't come. I did ask him a number of times. I begged him. But no, no. He wouldn't. 'Manchester?' he said.

Beatrice She exaggerates. Dublin people are excitable.

Anna Dublin. I used to dream of it. What is that softness of Dublin you dream of far away? Of course these country politicians have destroyed the old city, but what is that – that mystery which remains? The complete grace of it? The politeness of the servers in the shops, the lovely way older people have of greeting you. I don't care if young people think I'm mad to be a nun, or couldn't get a husband, or parts of me were sewn up, or whatever they think. That's all just temporary. We're a new nation now, and everything's being looked at. They're right, most of our old ways are antiquated. But they don't know yet that so many religious are looking at things anew and trying to adapt, and trying to get back . . . not the respect of the people, but the – you know, the feeling that a nun is a citizen too, a kind of fellow-worker. That she has a place. Oh, but this is my hobby horse. Nothing more tiresome, I know.

Beatrice You see, she exaggerates. The other day she said to me that nuns were like travellers, that you'd be refused a drink in a public house. I pointed out that she didn't drink anyway. Then she said we were like those boot-boys in the sixties. I must say I don't remember them. Then she said I was like an angel, given an off-putting human guise.

Anna I didn't mean off-putting, I meant . . .

Beatrice Vanity, I know.

Anna Everyone knows you're handsome, Beatrice.

Beatrice Handsome. Clark Gable was handsome. He had bad breath, did you know that?

Anna Well, anyway, I wrote to Mother Superior again and told her I was – you see, you have to write delicately to a Mother Superior, because they tend to see through everything, like Superman – I said I was concerned about Sister Beatrice's ulcers and could she be sent after me to Manchester, where there was this world-famous ulcer hospital, which there was. Mother wrote back saying she had looked into the matter and thought it best to keep Sister Beatrice in Ireland, where she was comfortable.

Beatrice If there'd been a world-famous ulcer hospital on Mars and Anna was there, I'd have risked the space rocket. What took them longest to work out was how to deal with the body waste of the astronauts. In the end they were told to go in their suits. Anything, anything to be with Anna.

Anna But it wasn't to be.

Beatrice No. Everything got worse. Mother Superior came to see me herself and asked me directly what the trouble was. She looked at me very closely, stared at me kind of, you know, entered my mind. Well, I couldn't tell her. I didn't know, I still don't. I was falling apart like an old pair of shoes. You don't like to tell your Mother Superior that you can't get by without – without Anna. It would have sounded so adolescent to her. She's a very distinguished woman, a Goldsmith scholar. My God. I much preferred to suffer in silence. Dignity, anyway.

Anna It was a sobering year for us.

Beatrice Then I was diagnosed diabetic. Pernicious something or other. The doctor looks at you sort of pityingly. I could have told him better. I was suffering from Annalessness, a little-known-and-understood disease. You could tell from the way he sat in the chair that he thought my career as a pernicious diabetic would be a short and glorious one. The needles were fun. Hatpins.

Anna When you think of the ignorance of the wise.

Beatrice To a degree. But management has to keep a certain detachment. After all, the business of the order couldn't be disrupted because two of us were – were – suffering. But then the lovely thing happened. Fred Astaire to the rescue.

Anna After a long time of misery, misery changes you. It adapts you to itself. As I came to the end of my time in England, I thought – this is it, they won't let me go home, they'll send me on now to Africa. And I would have gone . . .

Beatrice The Mother Superior turns up one day. I do remember it, I mean of course I remember it, but I remember it exactly, because it was a day when I thought I couldn't go on, I couldn't go on with those injections, feeling awful, passing out, being shunted in the ambulance to hospital every so often, all the wretched drama of the diabetic – and it was in that light of illness, a flickering rich sort of light – Mother Superior, a Leitrim woman, the most sensible person on earth, she comes in quietly and sits near me, and she recounts this dream. She'd had this dream the week before, and it was on her conscience, and she didn't understand it but she knew what she had to do. She'd had this dream where I was dancing with Anna, a slow immaculate dance, and Anna in a ball gown, and this clever Leitrim woman who never remembered her dreams ordinarily – wouldn't you think she'd be offended by such a dream, but no. She said no one knew the essence of things. Nobody, she says, can really say what represents what. What the meaning of things is, what the meaning of nuns is. She said it was her first and only vision, which she was going to nurture now for the rest of her life. She knew it was a good vision, she said. She knew there was something important in it, because when she cleared her mind it was still there, me and Anna dancing. So she was calling Anna Nagle home.

Anna So I came home.

Beatrice I thought I was going to die – from happiness, I mean. Not the diabetes or the ulcers. They just – fo, fiddle – vanished away. So that was Fred Astaire and Ginger Rogers.

Anna Fred Astaire and Jane Fonda, excuse me.

Beatrice I was so happy.

Anna makes a gesture with her arms, as if to say, 'And there you are.'